REACHING CLOUD 9

Surviving a Near-Death Skydive

2nd Edition

TYLER FARNHAM

Reaching Cloud 9 Second Edition

ISBN 978-1-943302-03-1

SECOND EDITION PRINTING: 2020

BEST SELLER BOOK DESIGN

BOOK DESIGN BY ADELE WIEJACZKA

PUBLISH@BESTSELLERBOOKDESIGN.COM

TYLER FARNHAM

TYLERFARNHAM.COM

ORDERING INFORMATION

SPECIAL DISCOUNTS ARE AVAILABLE ON QUANTITY PURCHASES BY CORPORATIONS, ASSOCIATIONS, EDUCATORS, AND OTHERS. FOR DETAILS, CONTACT THE PUBLISHER AT THE ABOVE LISTED ADDRESS.

BOOKING, PRESS & SPEAKING INQUIRIES

TYLERFARNHAM.COM/CONTACT

DEDICATION

None of my books would have come to life without the help of Dr. Michael Roych Lynch. Never have I had such an academic inspiration in my life... one who truly taught me many of life's lessons.

Not only were you my father's best friend, you were also mine.

We all love and miss you Big Mikey.

YESTERDAY IS HISTORY, TOMORROW IS A MYSTERY, AND TODAY IS A GIFT; THAT'S WHY THEY CALL IT THE PRESENT.

TABLE OF CONTENTS

SKYDIVER'S BRUSH WITH DEATH

Whole new life for broken man

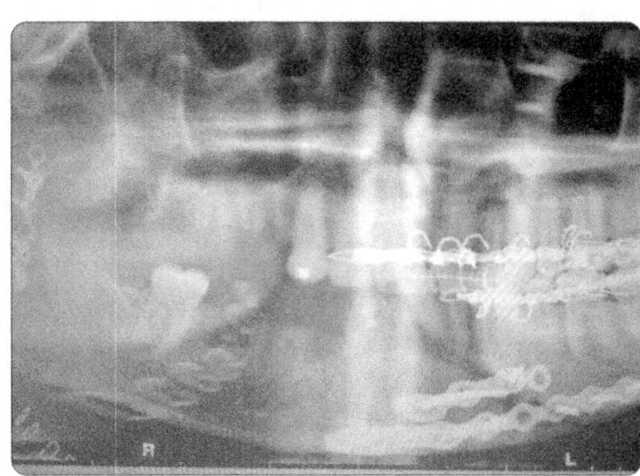

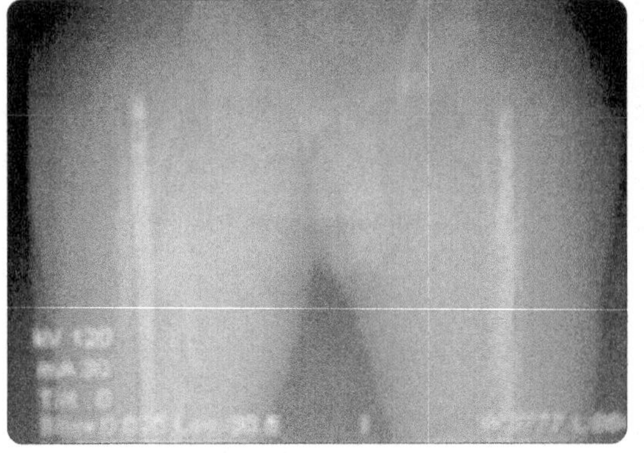

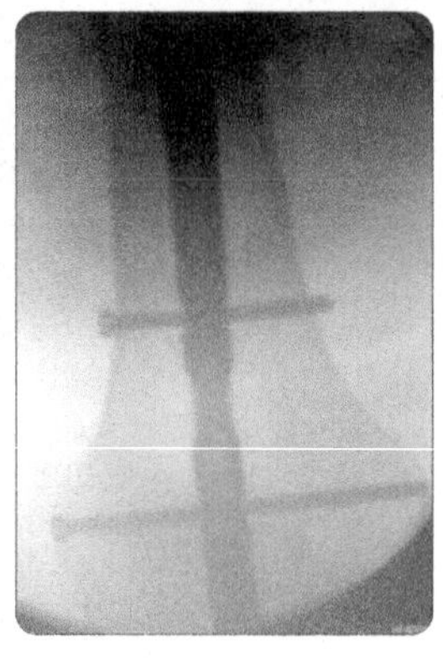

ACKNOWLEDGMENTS

MY BIGGEST THANKS TO ALL THOSE WHO WERE THERE FOR ME DURING A VERY DIFFICULT RIDE.

Jane Farnham
Kelly Farnham
Algee Family
Michael Royce Lynch
Jeff Scabarozi
Robert Turner
The Stewarts
Johan Compton
Josh Milstead
Mary and Morgan Rojas
Sharon Kline
Billy Knight
Brevard County Ocean Rescue
Skydive Sebastian
Cocoa Beach Pier
Ron Jon's Surf Shop
The Sandbar
Mark Farnham
Deb Guelzow
Lou Farnham
Garrett Lay
Dusty Scabarozi
Natalie Brace
Devin Cox
Lindsay Perry
TJ Corbin
Rick and Linda Musser
Jimmy Paine
Rob Stevenson
Brevard County Fire Rescue
Cocoa Beach Health and Fitness
Juice N Java
Longboard House

SPIRITUALITY, A BELIEF IN THE UNIVERSAL CONNECTION, OR THE GUIDING HAND OF A GREATER POWER ARE ALL SIGNIFICANT FACTORS IN OUR LIVES. THERE ARE OTHER FACTORS SUCH AS LEADERSHIP, PERSISTENCE AND HOPE THAT WE ALL NEED TO MEET LIFE'S CHALLENGES. TYLER'S STORY IS ONE OF GREAT DRAMA, SACRIFICE AND VICTORY. ALL OF US WILL FACE EXTREME CHALLENGES, BUT IT IS HOW WE SURVIVE AND RISE TO THE OCCASION THAT IS THE ESSENCE OF REACHING CLOUD NINE.

—MICHAEL LYNCH

VOLCOM

INTRODUCTION

Where do you see yourself in five years?

If someone were to have asked me this in 2008, I would have said, working as a firefighter in Cocoa Beach, Florida. Living near my parents, and maybe having a wife and kids.

Back then, I was working on the beach as a lifeguard captain, living with my best friends, dating a smoking hot girlfriend and was in school to become an EMT, which would further my career into the fire department.

I was not the same person as the one writing this now in my house while peering over a view of Gerupuk Bay in Lombok, Indonesia...I have changed, as we all do. More so I have evolved into someone different, as we all should.

To continue to evolve, grow and learn, I feel is the reason to be on this earth living this life. We make decisions that dictate our lives, and determine which paths we venture, when to take a shortcut or the path less traveled. Stay on the comfortable path, or take a chance, a risk? Maybe there is great rewards ahead. Sometimes there are mountains we must climb, and from the peak we can relish in our achievements. Spend time on this peak, enjoy, embrace, grow and learn. You will for sure meet others. There are the ones you left in the valley before you climbed the mountain who did not want to go with you. You meet some along the way, stuck, not wanting to continue the upward journey. You continue on... At the peak, you find some, happy and content with what they have found. Building a new life on this peak. But when you look into the distance, you see something new, something beautiful. Now you have to go down the mountain in order to reach that next peak.

On your downward journey, it is even more challenging. You lose loved ones, get injured, experience heartbreak. Should you continue on? You meet more people, ones on a similar journey. You share experiences from your last descent, you learn from one another. When you finally reach the valley, it is time to muster the courage and motivation to make the next climb. Climb again, meet others, gain knowledge, love, laugh... cry.

When you reach the top again, it is everything and more of what you imagined. Take your time to enjoy this before that next journey. Whereas now, you have learned to build a bridge across from peak to peak by using your past experiences and overcoming familiar challenges. There are those that travel the path and climb alone, and then there are those that go back down the mountain to bring others with them. Those are the leaders.

If you are constantly growing, learning and challenging yourself, this becomes a mild, and for some, intense form of addiction. Addiction to becoming a better person. Imagine you are a character in a movie, starring you. Take a look at where you are at. Look at your best friends, do you admire them, do they inspire you, are they leaders? What is it that you are after in life? There is a film crew documenting every moment... all your time. Are you in front of the TV or are you actually living? How would you turn it all around and become a true hero in your story? What kind of person do you want to be known as? We are not the same person we were yesterday... And if you are, ask yourself... Do you want to be different? Do you want to be better?

This is a story of my accident in 2009, how I got there and where it has left me, physically and mentally.

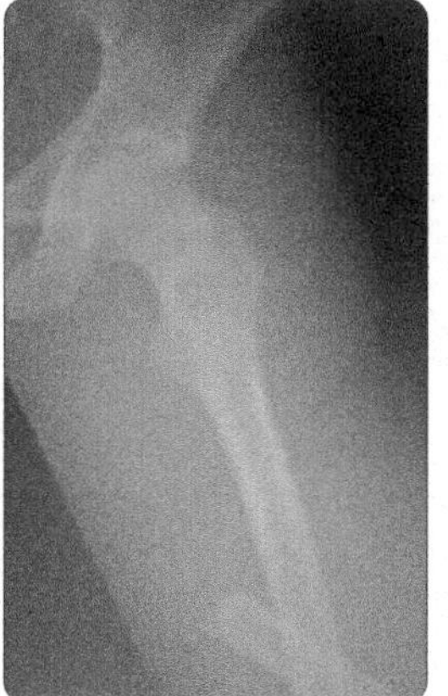
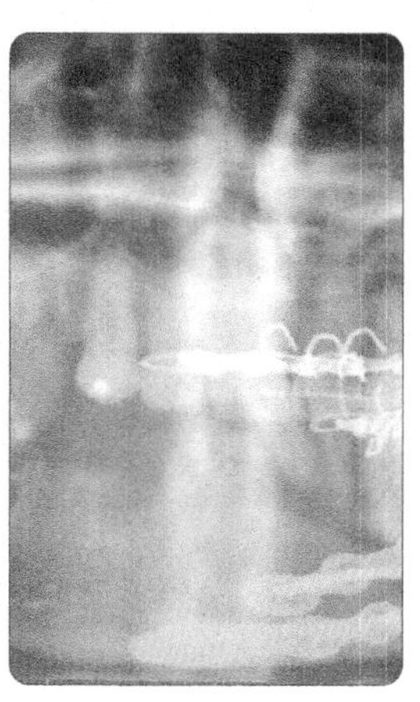

CHAPTER ONE

THE RHYTHM

When you live through a near death experience, life changes in many ways. All the small things in life that we as human beings take for granted, like walking and using our bodies, become very important. If you are capable of walking, then walk. If you can surf, then get out there and love every minute of it. If you are capable of jumping out of a perfectly good airplane, then jump. Life is all about living for today, in the present moment, not dwelling on the past. We cannot change the past and what may have changed our lives; accept the change and find the positives. Life can change in a matter of seconds, so cherish it. Every now and then I see someone in a wheelchair and it makes me think, what if that were me?

I am a strong believer in doing what you love. Being a professional surfer and traveling the world is, of course, most surfers' dream. That dream may come true only for a small handful, though. The rest of us have to make a living in the real world. We have to go to school, find a career and work nine to five Monday through Friday. This job has to support you, your wife, kids and, of course, the dog. This is the typical American dream. By no means is this a bad dream; I just happen to have a different one. Many people strive to make it to America. I do not blame them. America is a wonderful place with endless opportunities. But what else is out there? I think about it every day. I wonder what the typical day in Australia would be like. What is it like to wake up in Norway, have a cup of coffee, and jump off a cliff in a wingsuit and soar through the valleys. I have lived 27 wonderful years in a beautiful country but I cannot wait to see what else is out there.

I grew up in a small beach town on the East coast of Florida, Cocoa Beach. Miami sits four hours south, and Orland 45 minutes west. Orlando is known, of course, for Mickey Mouse and all of the other theme parks giving those roller coaster adrenaline hits to the majority of passing tourists. Miami is the party city with Cuban culture, Latino vibes and late nights. Cocoa Beach is known for two things, the Ron Jon surf shop and Kelly Slater, the 11-time surfing world champion.

My pops started pushing me into the waves by the age of three - surfing on my bright yellow Murray boogie board. Just a shy little kid who loved to surf and loved the ocean. I thought to myself, this is all I want to do; the best feeling ever was the feeling I got when surfing.

After surfing on my boogie board for the next couple of years, I finally decided I wanted a real surfboard. My dad knew that I was ready and was driven to get me one. He placed a bet on a Miami Dolphin game the summer of 89 with one of his buds, which he won, winning me a new Matt Keckly 5'5 Quiet Flight surfboard. The board was bright yellow, just like my boogie board. It had these bright neon colored zig zags, giving it a real 80s look. I loved that board more than anything.

My dad would push me into the waves in the beginning, when I was just learning, until I eventually started paddling out and catching waves on my own. I have memories of my dad standing on the shoreline, holding up his hand signaling to me, one more wave. That usually meant five more. He was interrupting my rhythm, and as a kid I did not think of time the way that my pops did, especially while surfing. But my dad knew, as all surfers know, time is viewed just a little bit differently in the ocean.

Growing up I always felt a strong difference when surfing alone versus surfing in a crowd. Surfers are versatile, and how they surf can reflect who they are as a person. Some like surfing in small groups, with friends, in pairs. Chatting in the lineup while waiting for waves, adding a social experience and sharing this feeling. Others, like me, love to surf alone—a wave of peace falls over me while I surf that is unexplainable, a form of meditation. There is a feeling of just you, your energy alone, in that moment of time, using the gift Mother Nature gave to those of us who choose to use it. This is the feeling that has kept me doing this for over 30 years.

Growing up in Florida, small surf is something you get used to, as you really have no choice. The beginning of June to the end of November is hurricane session. These are the months when Florida may experience heavy surf.

Storms start to brew in the Atlantic Ocean below Africa and gain strength, making their way to the Florida coastline. My small group of surfer friends, Ryan Jarrett and Mikey, would all surf together for years, learning how to read a variety of wave types, which would make us adaptable to different conditions throughout the years to come. But with Florida summer flat spells, skate-boarding often came first, my other passion.

When I was 14, I went on the road with my pops. He was a truck driver through-out my teenage years. It really was a great way to see the country, a teaser of what there was to go out and experience. From lush lakes to snow-capped mountains, we passed it all, and I got a good look at middle America, which really made me appreciate living in Florida.

Our final destination was Northern California. This would be my first experi-ence of the West Coast. At the time, I was skateboarding much more than I was surfing. As a kid I would go back and forth between the two, depending on whether I hung with my surfer or skater friends. The Atlantic Ocean also seemed to be closed to surfers most summers.

The reason for this cross country adventure was to skate Pier 7, which was one of the best skate spots in San Francisco, similar to what Hawaii is for surfing. This particular pier had different sets of stairs and cement block benches to do tricks on. My first day there, I was a little nervous considering the place was packed with talented locals, although eventually I eased into a good pace. After an hour or so, I was in the rhythm and did not even think of the other skaters. Looking back now, I remember it as one of the best skate sessions I have ever had. I remember having such a good run, landing every trick I attempted. Before I knew it, I had a couple good skaters sitting on one of the benches just watching me skate. My dad managed to video my whole session that day. As the day turned to early afternoon, the morning fog burned off. I skated for hours until I had no energy left. It was truly a day I will never forget. I found myself in the rhythm while skating many times in the past. But it was that day in San Francisco that is my most vivid memory of that feeling.

Those years we skated abandoned buildings, fast food restaurants, colleges... anywhere with stairs and handrails. Cops disliked us and our parents did not quite understand us. Those skate sessions were with the select few friends who had that similar taste, which was punk music and 411 skate videos. A lot of skaters are known as outcasts. Not really fitting into the normal team sports like baseball or football. I played soccer and baseball for years, but it was a different kind of lifestyle that I grew out of completely once I became a teenager. Skating and surfing were what I truly loved.

When I was 15, I had my first surf trip experience which was in Costa Rica. Inspired by the movie *Endless Summer 2*, I wanted to make a similar journey. This was my first trip out of the country and it gave me a true perspective of what it was like to surf heavier waves... I wanted more. Although I was working as a busboy at the Cocoa Beach Hilton, I did not know Spanish and I was not quite at that point in my life where I could relocate to a place like Costa Rica. From Jaco, Hermosa to Santa Teresa, I surfed alongside my dad while my grandmother sat patiently in the boat.

There is a common saying that refers to a surfer becoming addicted to waves, being bitten by the surfing bug. This happened to me on this trip. I was not so open to the culture, food or even the beautiful girls, it was only surfing. Arriving back home in Florida, the waves were flat with no sign of a swell. Unknowingly, I had my first taste of reverse culture shock. I got used to waking up every morning knowing I would have fun surf all day. Now it was the occasional waist-high crumbling waves, rather than the hollow, powerful Costa Rica surf.

I was so pumped and enlightened from the trip that I began surfing every day; even when it was flat I would just paddle out anyway, always in search of that feeling. Whether the surf was one foot or 10 feet, I was out. I began learning a bit of Spanish to prepare for my next trip to Central America. I did not keep the momentum though. Looking back I can see if I would have, I could have been a master in Spanish. Back then, I did not understand the importance of such a skill. When I was 16 and had my drivers license, I began skipping Spanish classes and driving to the beach to go surfing instead, surfing was still my main priority.

All I watched were surf videos during those years. Before paddling out with my friends, we would watch a video to get pumped up, hyped before the surf. It was our hometown hero, Kelly Slater, along with the Lopez brothers and Hobgoods, who were the local inspirations to surfers in Florida back then. They gave us all hope that we could become the new generation of talent and motivated us to keep progressing. Unfortunately drugs took down many of those up-in-comers in the later years.

There were other surfers I idolized besides the Florida guys. Taylor Knox and Chris Ward were California surfers that also played a role in motivating all of us throughout the 90s. All the music in the videos was the music I grew up listening to, anything from Pennywise to Strung Out to Bad Religion. The music played a massive role in motivating me to keep doing this, day after day, and it continues to do so today.

I have spoken to a lot of people about how surfing can be an analogy for life. You constantly chase that feeling of surfing a wave. But you must paddle back out and get back to the peak, which takes hard work, heavy breathing and drive. How much can you endure? I have taught surfing for a number of years, and when I can bring someone into the ocean with me, paddle with them, guide them on the peak and watch the expression on their face when they ride the wave, it always makes me smile.

Surfing really defines who I am as a human being. I was the kid who spent every day at the beach. I cannot help but think, maybe I was visualizing, or as my teachers called it, daydreaming, all throughout my childhood of being in a place where I could capture that feeling, the feeling only surfing gives me.

CHAPTER TWO

MOTIVATIONAL DRIVE

"MUSIC, AT ITS ESSENCE, IS WHAT GIVES US MEMORIES. AND THE LONGER A SONG HAS EXISTED IN OUR LIVES, THE MORE MEMORIES WE HAVE OF IT."

—STEVIE WONDER

Growing up—and even now—I listen to music every single day of my life. The feelings created by music are strong enough to open up doors to memories from the past. Sometimes these memories are happy, funny, sad... sometimes very sad. This is something very powerful that can really impact your life in a positive way when used correctly. A single melody can change the way you feel—from being sad to happy. People have different styles, or shall I say genres, of music that make them feel good. A song or artist I do not care for could be someone else's everything. It took me a long time, and a lot of growing up, to realize that something I really do not like could mean so much to someone else.

My memories of music go back to when I was just a kid, living at home with my sister, Kelly. The door to my room was covered with album covers of different artists from the early 90s. I used a black sharpie to coat my door with names of artists like Nirvana, Pearl Jam, and Soundgarden. Being a young teenager, I idolized these bands and their songs. Different songs and melodies trigger different human emotions. That is the beauty of music; if you are having a bad day, music can cure your sadness.

Born in the 80s, my era of music began in the early 90s with grunge. Sometimes called the Seattle sound, grunge music started in the mid-80s. The independent record label Sub Pop is what got the ball rolling for grunge in Seattle, Washington. *Entertainment Weekly* called grunge, "the biggest exploitation of a subculture since the media discovered hippies in the '60s." With its unique style, almost a lazy appearance, the genre was all about flannels and clothing from thrift stores. It was no surprise that the outcast skater kids fell heavily into this scene, as they could relate to the feeling that they got from the music. Since the genre was Seattle-based, so were a lot of the artists.

Nirvana was an American rock band started by Kurt Cobain and Krist Novoselic. It originated in the small town of Aberdeen, Washington. Nirvana's album "Nevermind" is what really got the scene going along with Pearl Jam's album "Ten." Pearl Jam was another Seattle-based band that really got noticed for their unique sound. It was bands like Black Sabbath and Led Zeppelin that shaped the sound of grunge. The lyrics mainly addressed the issues of social alienation, apathy and a desire for freedom. These bands were a music following for youth.

It was not until the mid-90s that these artists became very well known and grunge was born. By Christmas of 1991, Nirvana's "Nevermind" was selling four hundred thousand copies a week. By 1992, "Nevermind" made number one on the top 200 billboard, beating Michael Jackson's "Dangerous." These bands were becoming very recognized and popular. At this time I was only eight years old and I already had a strong passion for music, with my CD collection continuously growing. Throughout my life, music would become my most important luxury.

Grunge music was short-lived but made its impact on the music scene. I was too young to really understand the politics of music and what some of the lyrics meant. To lots of kids, music was their escape and still is—whether it was a broken home, trouble at school, whatever it may have been. Music was an outlet for kids who needed a positive path to follow. For me, my love for music was not due to a need for a life direction, but simply because it gave me a feeling of pure happiness.

As I grew through my teen years I did listen to what was popular at the time. Grunge music eventually died out and then it was hip hop that was in. I still had the love for Pearl Jam and Nirvana, along with many other bands, but it was now time to start new memories. Along with my friends, I started listening to artists like Tupac Shakur and Notorious B.I.G.. These two artists created a revolution in the hip hop community. Tupac's songs were about growing up in the ghetto, racism and gang violence, something I knew nothing about, but I liked the beats. My interest in hip hop music was short-lived due to the fact that it did not motivate me like other music genres.

Every band has its prime. Once that initial hype wears off, it is off to the next big sound. After high school, I went straight back to my roots—alternative punk. My initial liking of bands like Pennywise and Strung Out came from 90s surf videos. The music fit so perfectly with surfing that it made me want to find similar artists. Around that time in my life, my buddy Rob moved in across the street.

We started listening to newer punk bands like Billy Talent and Riverboat Gamblers, and bands that started the punk revolution like the Ramones and Minor Threat. The Clash and the Sex Pistols were the first UK punk bands with a similar sound. These bands sang about being different or social conflicts. Society did not know how to react to this type of music. It was poppy and fast, and had a unique style. Music influences for the Ramones were the Rolling Stones, the Beach Boys, the Beatles, and similar bands from the 50s and 60s.

My first concert was a memorable one. I was 15 years old and was with my high school buddy, Eric. The bands playing were Mustard Plug and Less Than Jake, both ska bands. Ska is a genre of music that was developed in Jamaica in the 50s. The concert was held at the Hilton in Indialantic on a boardwalk along the beach. The place was packed. I knew about Mustard Plug but had not heard much of their music. Less Than Jake, on the other hand, was one of my favorite bands at that time. Once Less Than Jake took the stage, the crowd went wild. I recognized every song. With the energy, I felt I wanted to be as close to the stage as possible. This was an urge to move fast, a form of dancing to this style of music. It was a build up of adrenaline.

The term for what I was about to experience is known as moshing. Moshing is what fans do at live performances to release energy generated by the music. It is a way to express your energy and love for the music through jumping around and bouncing off other fans. Some take it to the extreme and become violent. That is the downfall of moshing. Some bands like the Smashing Pumpkins are anti-moshing due to the injuries, and some reported deaths, from this expression of enjoyment. To some it may seem childish or just plain ridiculous, but for the music lover it is a form of dancing and expression of passion for the music in that particular moment.

It was much later in life, the summer of 2010 when my best buddy Garrett introduced me to The Drums. The Drums are a band from New York with a much different sound that I was used to. This was a sound that in the past years I would never have given a chance. Along with The Drums, Garrett also shared with me Surfer Blood and Wavves. At first I was only into a few of these bands' songs. Soon they became all I would listen to.

In March of 2011, Garrett, myself and our buddy Chuck flew to Austin for a music festival, South by Southwest. South by Southwest is a weeklong festival for up-and-coming bands, which play across multiple venues. This is the place to be to witness the next big thing in music. We must have seen close to fifty different shows during our five days in Austin. We witnessed amazing new bands, along with some familiar ones. This was when I found a new passion, music festivals.

Arriving back to Florida, Garrett had heard that Surfer Blood was doing a show in Athens, Georgia. He mentioned that he would go if I were game to road trip it with him. The only problem was that I had to be at work the next morning at 9 a.m. sharp. With a strong desire to see the show, we made the trip with our two friends, Natalie and Erica. As soon as the show ended we drove right back to Florida, just in time for me to make it to work.

This was not the first and certainly would not be the last time I would go to such lengths for music. From Spain, Sweden, Australia and New Zealand to a one night stay in Kuala Lumpur, I have made long journeys for shows. The memories that you get from these shows, these experiences, combined with the emotions that come along with the music, are priceless. This is future fuel for inspiration, simply looking back and remembering the feeling from the last experience can change your mind and mood in just moments.

I often go into deep thought when I listen to music. That is what triggers all the memories when you are truly tuned in. All those emotions you were feeling the first time you heard that song come back every time you listen to it. I have had to stop listening to many artists throughout my life because of the sad memories of my first true love flooding back into my thoughts. Still today, music provides my main drive to do everything in my daily life from working out to surfing to writing... everything. The flow of productivity is constant with just the right melodies. I often view my music as a timeline of my life. Along with my journals, I can look back and listen to music to relive memories, good bad and sad, to see how I got to where I am today.

CHAPTER THREE

THE ADRENALINE HITS

"OTHER GUYS SNORT FOR IT, JAB A VEIN FOR IT. ALL YOU GOTTA DO IS JUMP."

—BODHI

> "As I approached the door I felt the wind rushing at me so fast. My adrenaline was pumping so I was not even fazed one bit by the cold. Once at the edge of the door I looked down. BJ was no longer in sight, I just saw clouds and earth. We stood in the doorway about five seconds before diving out of the plane. Instantly I had this dropping feeling of my stomach in my throat."

Music and movies inspire hundreds of thousands of people to do what they love and chase their dreams. My inspiration came when I was a little kid, and the movie *Point Break* was released. This soon became my all-time favorite film. The premise of the movie is about surfing and skydiving in Southern California. A small group of friends want to live an endless summer. To do so, they surf, skydive and rob banks to fund their lifestyles. Patrick Swayze and Keanu Reeves star in the movie. I became fixated with this movie and the lives these guys were living. I was so intrigued by skydiving that it became something I had to try.

April 2001 marked my 18th birthday. My two buddies, Eric and BJ, were going skydiving with me. This was something I had waited 10 long years for, and the time was finally here. So we all packed into my little Mercury Sable and began our drive to Skydive Sebastian. The drive took roughly an hour, with lots of mixed emotions along the way.

We pulled up to the drop zone, and that is when we all got a little nervous. We were here and the reality had set in. There were two hangers, with one side for packing parachutes, and the other for check in and what is known as a rigging loft. This is the area where the rigger packs the reserve canopies. There were also many different rooms on this side. One room was where all the instructors prepared and edited their tandem videos. I noticed another room that skydive students were coming in and out of. This was the equipment room with all the student parachutes, helmets and jumpsuits. It was years later when I first entered some of these rooms.

Just south of the hangers, there was a store called the Drop Shop that sold new and used skydiving gear. Next to the Drop Shop was the Zoo Bar and Restaurant. All along its walls were pictures of various skydivers and formation jumps. I was reminded of a scene from *Point Break* where Johnny Utah is at Bodhi's house looking at all his photos on the wall of anything from surfing to rock climbing to skydiving. I did not realize it then, but I was jumping at one of the most popular, well-known drop zones in the world.

On the other side of the hangers was an area for training, which included various classrooms and showers. This was where students going through the Accelerated Freefall Course (AFF) would spend most of their time training. The main drop zone had multiple taxiways for airplanes and a few fields for the skydivers to land. The main spot for landing was right in front of the hangers with a small rock pile called the peas. This is meant to be the bull's eye for landing, and where most instructors would touch down.

After standing around for a few minutes watching the jumpers and just checking the place out, we were approached by our instructors. I was jumping with Uwe. I could not place where he was from, but definitely not the United States. Eric and BJ were met by their instructors, and we immediately began going over the skydive. The briefing lasted all of maybe five to 10 minutes. They told us, "Once we are at 10,000 feet, we are going to strap you to the harness that's on the instructor." All of us were getting videoed, so they were asking us on the ground in the hanger if we were excited and why we decided we wanted to try skydiving. Today, it is really funny to watch the video and see all of us trying so hard not to look nervous.

Everything seemed to happen so quickly. First, came a briefing from our tandem instructors, then being harnessed up. The harness fit snugly around our shoulders and thighs. It had metal clips attached, which hooked into the instructor's harness. "I will lock you into my harness at around 10,000 feet." This was the last thing my instructor said to me before exiting the hanger. Right outside the hanger was a concrete pad with a picnic table and some chairs for spectators. A fence separated the pad from the taxiway. There were random signs on the fence like, "Propellers chop off heads" and "No Spectators Beyond This Point."

From there we walked north along the fence past the packing hanger and through a grass field toward the plane. In the middle of the grass field was a section of a plane. It was meant to simulate the inside of a plane. This was here for jumpers to practice their exits, especially for students and large groups. As we approached the real plane, the engine started up. We walked around the plane from the back and one by one the jumpers crawled in. My buddies and I were last to enter the plane, all being filmed while doing so. We were all packed in like sardines; each jumper would sit back with their legs open so the next could sit in front of them. This was the most efficient way to pack everyone in.

As we started down the runway, my instructor advised me to look at the flags in the field to determine wind direction. It is crucial to know the wind direction prior to even getting on the airplane, but it may change so it pays to be aware. As we took off, a couple people hooted and hollered. The plane seemed to shake and dip quite a bit during the takeoff, which I figured was typical; at least I hoped it was. As far as jumping out of a perfectly good airplane, not sure. On our ride to altitude, our cameramen would randomly ask us questions and film outside the plane. One of the cameramen shut the door shortly after takeoff, then reopened it once we took off our seatbelts at 2,000 feet. The temperature had already dropped significantly.

After the cameraman got some good footage of the inlet, they shut the door for the rest of the ride up to altitude. BJ would be going first, followed by myself and then Eric. There were some small groups of fun jumpers that would be exiting before us, considering they would pull lower than us. Just as they said, at 10,000 feet we had to get harnessed up to our instructors.

Once the plane reached altitude, it stalled to slow down. The door was pulled open and very chilly wind flooded the cabin. I was behind BJ, but I could still see a few jumpers waiting to exit before him. It looked surreal seeing people jump out of a plane first hand. The plane jerked a bit each time someone would exit, due to losing weight. Once BJ was up, his camera guy climbed out of the plane and stood on the camera step just outside the exit door. BJ and his instructor approached the door, and then head first seemed to just fall right out. The most intense part for me was seeing my buddy just dive out of the plane right in front of me, knowing I was next. As I approached the door, I felt a strong rush of wind. My adrenaline was pumping, so I was not fazed one bit by the cold. Once at the edge of the door, I looked down. BJ was no longer in sight; I just saw clouds and earth.

We stood in the doorway for around five seconds before diving out of the plane. Instantly I had this dropping feeling of my stomach in my throat, plummeting head first toward the earth at a speed of over 100 miles an hour. Once I gained my composure, Uwe tapped my shoulder, which was a signal for me to uncross my arms and let them out to my sides. By this time we were falling at 120 miles an hour. Our cameraman approached us and extended his hand. I grabbed onto it and we began to spin. I was in awe of the view and the feeling of falling. The day was gorgeous, with white puffy clouds and bright blue sky. The ocean was turquoise and the inlet was absolutely breathtaking. That first time, everything happens so quickly that it was over before I even realized it. The whole free fall lasted 60 seconds, then Uwe pointed to the ripcord, my signal to pull. Our canopy opened, no problems.

While under the canopy, I began asking Uwe questions about the sport and how to progress to solo jumps. He informed me of the AFF program. At 4,000 feet, he let me take the toggles and fly the canopy. Once we dropped to just a few thousand feet, Uwe took them back and started doing some intense turns. I felt that falling feeling a couple more times under the canopy until a couple of thousand feet. That is when Uwe focused on our landing area and eased up on the turns. He instructed me to lift my legs up until he said stand up. It seemed we were coming in fast until he pulled on the brakes and then we just eased to the ground. "Stand up!" We had touched down and collapsed our canopy.

As soon as my feet hit the ground, I felt this burst of adrenaline come over me. I thanked my instructor and thanked Scott, my camera guy. Eric was already grounded and out of his harness. I gave him a big hug and the two of us were ecstatic. I knew right then that I wanted to be a skydiver.

I was so thrilled with skydiving after my first jump, it was all I could think about. My main love was, and would always be, surfing. Considering it is flat so many months out of the year, I needed another hobby. I had stopped skateboarding a few years back due to injuries and a shift of friends, so it seemed that skydiving would take on this new role.

I knocked out two more tandems within the first year and so did Eric. Those tandems were very beneficial. The first skydive is pure excitement but nerve-wracking. After that you can focus on the big picture and what is really going on. Eric had really enjoyed skydiving too and decided to get certified with me.

The AFF consists of eight levels or jumps. First you must complete ground school, a four-to-six-hour class where you learn all the basics. This is where you go over all the equipment and how it works. Learn how to fly stable with body movement and control. One of the tools is a large box on wheels with a soft pad on top. You would lay on this box on your belly with your back arched and arms out at 90 degrees. Your legs would be slightly bent at the knees and slightly arched up. We would learn about emergency landings, key altitudes, malfunctions and cutaways. We were then taken over to a harness suspended in the air from a wooden platform. The idea was for each of us, one at a time, to get harnessed in and actually perform the cut away procedure. "Peel out, punch, pull!"

This was what we were taught to shout over and over again to lock it into our brains if we had to cut away. The procedure was to look, locate your cut away handle and reserve handle, and grasp them both. With your right hand, peel up and punch out the cut away handle. Then, immediately using your left hand, pull your reserve handle; this would pull a pin which would deploy your reserve canopy. Then you would arch your back and prepare for deployment.

After getting the feel of cutting away, we moved on to the next drill. One by one we would sit in a chair and verbalize our deployment procedure. The instructor would hold a picture of a canopy over our head. Sometimes it would be a square, steerable, stable parachute. Then at other times it would be a picture of either a low-speed or high-speed malfunctioning parachute. Our job would be to verbalize what actions we would take in case of a malfunction. We would have to act quickly, especially in the case of a high-speed malfunction considering that you are still falling at over 100 miles an hour. One of the malfunctions is called a bag lock. This is when your parachute does not come out of the deployment bag. There really is nothing you can do but cut away. Seconds are crucial when in a situation like this; you must act quickly and make the right choices. It may save your life.

Your first three jumps are with two instructors, one on either side of you. The next five you do with only one instructor who critiques you. Each level builds on the last, teaching you new skills. There are objectives that go with each jump, which must be met in order to move on to the next level. You have a one-way radio strapped to your chest for the instructor to talk you through the landing from the ground. The eighth and final jump is called a hop and pop. This jump consists of jumping from the plane at 5,500 feet, which is your pull altitude as a student, getting stable and pulling. This is your graduation jump. If you land short of the drop zone, you land on the beer line. This means you buy the instructors a case of beer. This is one of the rules at Skydive Sebastian.

The whole program can be completed in three or four days depending on your budget, skill level and the weather. If a task is not performed correctly, you may have to redo a jump. A lot of students end up practicing in the wind tunnel located in Orlando. We were both completely hooked on skydiving, and at this time in my life I had put surfing on the backburner.

My first solo skydive was intense. In the plane on the way up, I had to verbalize the whole skydive from start to finish to my instructors. Once at altitude, after getting a final gear check, I stood at the exit door and checked in with each instructor to get the okay to exit. Once cleared to jump, I made the plunge. For the first few jumps, you are joined by two instructors, one on either side. They are watching your every move while correcting you and guiding you using hand signals to communicate . You are taught to stay arched through the beginning of the skydive; this keeps you flying belly to the earth in a stable condition. It is easy to lose control of your body position during those first few skydives; this is what your instructors are there for.

Once in a stable free fall, you must perform maneuvers. You are given a syllabus at the beginning of the course with instructions for each dive. During the first skydive, you do not have many exercises to execute. Considering this is your first solo skydive, they do not want to overwhelm you. Your goals for this first skydive are to stay altitude aware and perform practice pulls. At 6,000 feet, I would lock eyes on my altimeter and once at 5,500 feet I would pull. After deploying my canopy, I felt an enormous rush. I did not let this stop me from doing what I was taught. I immediately looked up at my canopy to ensure there were no problems. I had a one-way radio with my instructor who was directing my turns. I stuck around my holding area and flew my wind pattern as directed. My whole skydive was routine, no problems.

After reaching the ground, Eric and I would each get debriefings from our instructors, critiquing us on the whole dive from start to finish. We were issued log books to document our progress and keep track of our jumps. After the first skydive, we had seven more to complete. The next six were all different, all including exercises from turns to forward speed, flips, slow fall/fast fall and tracking. Tracking is the term given to flying with forward speed. This can be done by even the most amateur skydivers, but it takes lots of practice to be a good tracker. Every maneuver that is executed is not meant to look pretty, but to show the instructors that you are able to stabilize after throwing your body into different positions going over 100 miles an hour.

Eric and I completed our AFF course in three weeks. My seventh jump was videoed so we could run through it to prepare for my eight and final jump, the hop and pop. I executed everything just fine, with a clean opening and good landing. Eric and I graduated from the accelerated free fall program in early August of 2001.

After graduating, the next step was to become a licensed skydiver. This would be done after completing 25 jumps, taking a written test as well as an accuracy test and last, packing and jumping a student canopy. Being an A licensed jumper meant you could jump at any drop zone in the United States. Already having eight jumps logged meant I just had to put the time in and start jumping as much as possible. Any time I would have a day off, I would head south with Eric to Sebastian. Eventually Eric slowed down on his jumping due to his hectic work schedule. I worked my way up to 25 jumps within the next six months but did not attempt to acquire the license.

There are three kinds of skydivers. First there are the jump junkies. These are the ones who quit their jobs and either get a job at a drop zone, or just spend every dime they have on jumping. They basically live at the drop zone and live to skydive. Next are the weekend warriors. This group works outside the airport and once the weekend hits, it is jump time. They still maintain a life outside skydiving, but it is a big part of it. Last are the ones who jump a couple times a month to stay current, and to get the thrill of these 60 second rides of their lives. Skydiving is still a big part of their lives, but life gets in the way of committing 100 percent. I fall into this category.

Shortly after I started skydiving in 2001, I came across BASE jumping. BASE is an acronym for buildings, antennas, spans (bridges) and earth (cliffs). The biggest difference between BASE jumping and skydiving is that in BASE jumping, you only have one parachute. Also, instead of having a free fall altitude of 13,000 feet, in BASE jumping you may only have 1,000 feet. Mistakes can easily cost you your life. Packing, canopy control and quick thinking are all imperative in this sport. There is a BASE jumping camp in Idaho where you can learn the basics such as packing, jumping and canopy control. Norway is the hot spot for BASE, just like Hawaii is for surfing. I had intentions of making it to that point, to jump off a mountain was what I really wanted to do. I was always chasing that next best high in life.

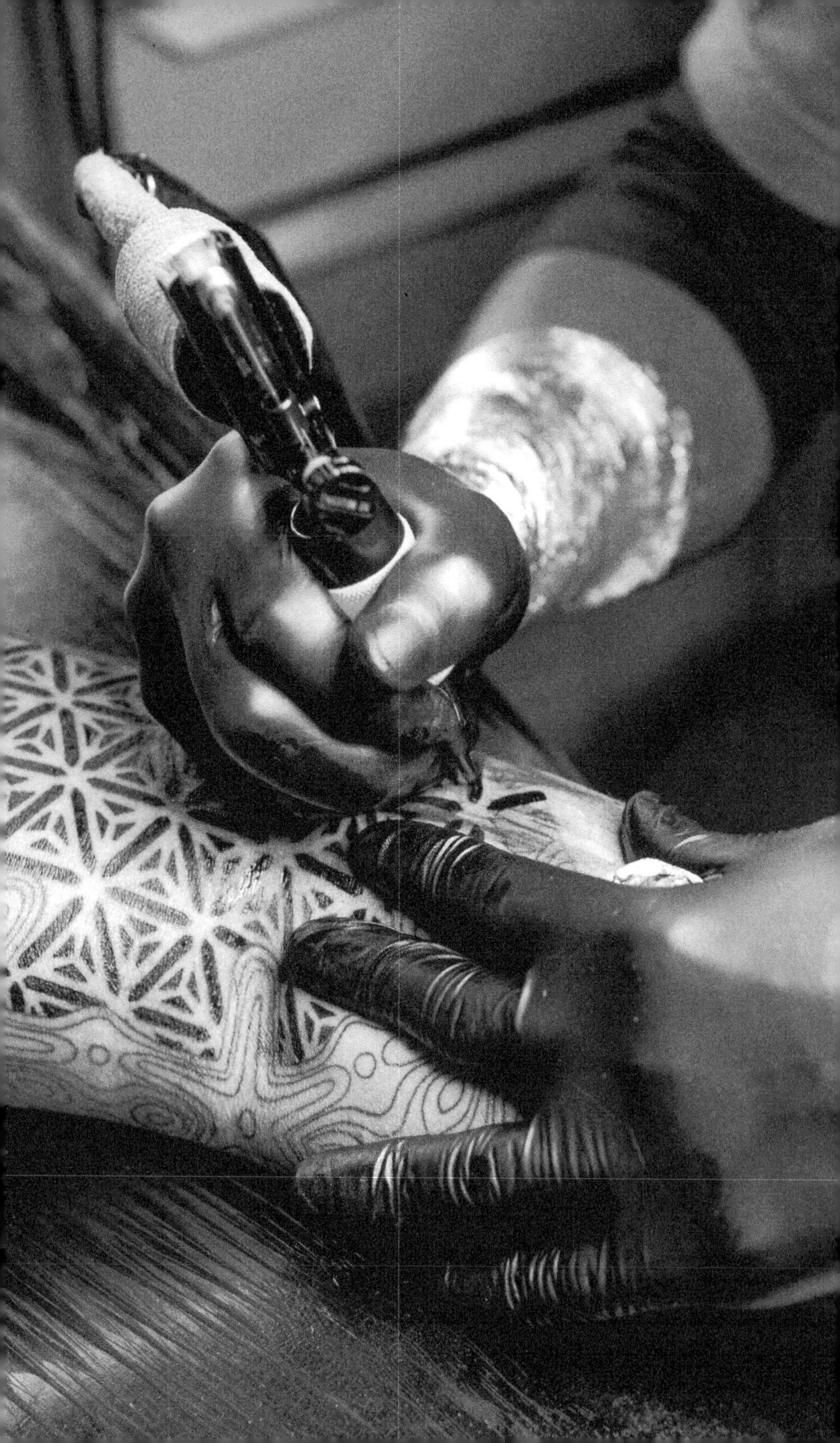

CHAPTER FOUR

PERSONAL DEVELOPMENT

"LIFE ISN'T ABOUT FINDING YOURSELF. LIFE IS ABOUT CREATING YOURSELF."

—GEORGE BERNARD SHAW

I was 19 when I started getting tattoos. I was influenced by my buddy, Rob, who would always stop by my house and show off his newest artwork. The shop he used was Artistic Bodyworks, right next door to Ron Jon's surf shop. At first I only wanted to get one tattoo. This quickly changed, as I ended up getting addicted to not just the new art, but the experience of being in the shop. The sounds, smells, pain and conversations with the artists... the ritual.

From there I started seeing an artist who went by the name Ghost. I would sit with Ghost, and go over ideas and drawings. These were all works of art, and they all reflected my lifestyle and connection with the ocean.

I had been going to school at Brevard Community College, working towards an associate's degree. I really had no idea what I wanted to do with my life. Most kids turn towards the military when they do not have a solid life plan. Well, that is what I ended up doing; I decided I wanted to join the Coast Guard. This would be a great way to make a living, travel and see the world. After getting a tour at Port Canaveral, I went to visit a recruiting office. I soon learned that tattoos were heavily frowned upon, not only in the Coast Guard, but in the Air Force and the Navy, which were the only branches of the military I had an interest in. I had no choice but to return to school and continue on in Brevard County.

Once I became a regular at Artistic, I got a piece from one of the other artists. While he was tattooing me, he told me about this website called Myspace. I decided I would check it out for myself. This was when Myspace was just beginning and was somewhat new to the world. I went ahead and put together a profile and started meeting a lot of girls. This was inevitable due to all the other young people discovering this site for social networking. It must have only been a couple of weeks before I met Britney from California. My skydiving pictures were what sparked the conversation. We began chatting quite often. I would tell her about my skydives and life in Florida, and she would share her life as a makeup artist on the West Coast. We continued talking on the phone for a couple of months before she invited me to visit her in L.A. Within a couple weeks I was on a plane.

Britney was your typical California girl. She was 5'2" with long dark hair and a West Coast mentality, which ultimately drew me in. She picked me up from LAX and gave me the grand tour of her hometown in Santa Clarita Valley. We had spoken so much over the phone that we felt like we already knew each other. We stayed at her condo the first couple of days, and she took me to all the usual tourist spots in Hollywood, as well as Malibu and Venice Beach. Then we decided on a whim to drive to Vegas. We stayed in Caesars Palace for a night. The night consisted of a long hot bath, copious amounts of alcohol and what almost resulted in a wedding. We then drove to meet her aunt and cousins in Phoenix. Britney's aunt was a student advisor at the Arizona Automotive Institute (AAI). At the time, I was enrolled at the Marine Mechanics Institute in Orlando where I was learning about marine diesels. I figured it would be easy to back out of school in Orlando and enroll in Glendale, Arizona, to learn the same skill but with auto diesel engines. After discussing our options and confessing our love for each other, we had to act on it. The plan was to move to Arizona, attend AAI and then move to San Diego after finishing school. When you are young, you sometimes make irrational decisions. This was mine.

We tend to make spontaneous decisions when we are in love, or think we are in love. Being young, those decisions can really dictate the direction your life takes, along with future decisions. This was the first time I left my comfort zone of Cocoa Beach. The move was in some ways difficult due to the fact that I was leaving everything I knew – the ocean, the house I grew up in and all my friends. But the adventure seemed like a good idea, at the time at least.

For the most part I just up and left. I only told a few of my closest friends and then just skipped town. I was at a loss about my future, and I do believe that I thought that this escape from my home town would enable me to live happily ever after in Southern California. My sister, Kelly, drove with me in my '99 Dodge Ram, packed with all my gear in the bed of the truck, in pursuit of this new life.

Adjusting to Arizona was difficult, which I never really took into consideration before I left. I did not have the ocean across the street to rely on when I needed it. I also did not have a job, and was about to embark on my new school year and career. I began hunting for jobs almost immediately once Britney and I were settled. I was going to restaurants looking for a serving or bartending gig. My problem was not lack of experience, but once again the tattoos. Any restaurant with a short-sleeved uniform was out. That is when I narrowed it down to restaurants whose servers wore long sleeves. My first stop was Carrabba's Italian Grill on Bell Road. I sat down with the proprietor Chris and had what seemed to be a great interview. I told him this would be my first job waiting tables. This worked to my advantage since Carrabba's liked to hire those new to serving—no bad habits to break. Just like that, I got the job. I went from running food to shadowing trainers. Within a week I was on the floor...

When the weekend came, it was off to San Diego. This was the main reason for moving—having access to the best waves in the states. Not mentioning that I thought I had met the love of my life. The first couple drives to Cali were not bad, but each five-hour drive would get longer and longer. The prize at the end of Interstate 8, however, was always well worth it.

The most important thing at the time was having a steady job, and I had one. I have worked many restaurants back in Florida, but only as a busser, never a server. I caught on quickly and enjoyed the company of my co-workers. This was also when I truly saw growth in my people skills, being social with new people every night. Having to approach couples, families and large groups, I would constantly, night after night, have to in some ways befriend all those I came in contact with. This broke me out of my shy teenage years.

Once school started at AAI, I quickly realized how different I was from everyone else. Most of my classmates were already working in the field. I was the only student in the whole school who had a surfer magazine and read it most of the day, between and sometimes during classes. I struggled to pay attention; with California only five hours away, I often found myself in a surfing dream world instead of giving my full attention in class. My childhood was the beach and surfing, not mechanics. Lots of kids growing up learn how to change oil and rotate tires from their fathers. I never had that interest, so I never had the practice. Early on I began asking myself, "What am I doing here?" "Have I made the right choice?" Making these kind of choices in our early 20s, to me now sounds foolish. I believe that the majority of kids coming out of high school need to have multiple experiences before making a decision about what they want to do with the rest of their lives as adults. You may discover new talents and have new visions after you leave school. For me, I felt pressure being surrounded by classmates that leapt into college right out of high school. Either they had good grades and got scholarships, or they did the same as me and started in a community college before progressing to higher education. I struggled with math, which kept me from progressing with my AA degree. After getting rejected by the Coast Guard, I thought a trade would be a good choice. I had a small sum of money left to me by my grandmother, which would partially help me live. My mom helped me with the student loans, which would stick with us for the rest of our lives thanks to the corrupt U.S. educational system.

I felt like I had to follow through with my decision. I was not working in the field I was studying. I made good money waiting tables, and I just figured I would graduate and find a job soon after. Our trips to Cali were fun; we stayed at Britney's grandfather's house in Santa Clarita Valley, right outside L.A. I got to surf and I had a tour guide who was knowledgeable about the area and was not bad to look at either. It was all good, except for going back to Phoenix. I began to dislike where I lived and deeply missed the ocean. Skydiving felt like plummeting into a hot oven so I did not experience the same feelings I had when skydiving in Florida. I had jumped into a decision to move to the desert, not thinking logically. My relationship with Britney was withering due to not being happy with my surroundings. This was a new place; I gave it a shot and decided quite early on that I wanted out.

It had been roughly three months of living in Phoenix when Britney and I split. She moved out of our apartment, taking all of her furniture and leaving me in an empty condo. We had rushed into what seemed like a good thing. After really getting to know each other, we both realized we had made a big mistake. When you are young, sometimes you have to live through an experience and learn from it. This seemed to be a trend for me throughout life. The school was only 14 months long; I had only a year to go. If it were not for my friends at

Carrabba's donating furniture and just being there for me, it would have been more difficult than it already was.

Britney's cousin, Josh, began coming out to Cali with me and I would teach him how to surf. Back in Phoenix, Josh would teach me how to ride and jump BMX bikes, a short-lived skill for me. BMX, along with wakeboarding, gave me a feeling that somewhat resembled the one surfing gave me, a form of adrenaline rush in the desert. Josh also introduced me to Todd. Todd ran a very lucrative pool business, in which Josh was his second hand man. I began working with the two of them, and every Friday had my pool route of 22 pools to clean in the suburbs of Phoenix. My co-workers at Carrabba's were all becoming good friends. Once I found personalities that I found authentic, I got myself into a bit of a pattern. We would go across the street every night after work to a bar called Famous Sam's and shoot pool. Late nights were normal, and early on I found myself in the hospitality world where maybe I experienced the most of my personal growth up to that time of my life. Skating the pool daily, keeping the pace at school and finding my rhythm going through this chapter of my life, I was in many ways happy.

Shortly after my breakup with Britney, my friend and fellow co-worker, John, had introduced me to one of his friends, Courtney. Courtney and I soon became close and started dating. She was an Arizona native and one of the sweetest girls I had ever met. About 5'7," with long brown hair, she was absolutely stunning. Just a few weeks after we started dating, she flew back to Florida with me to meet my friends and family. She was genuine and had a good heart, the exact opposite of Britney. I do believe that once I was surrounded by the co-workers that I soon would call friends, I felt comfortable enough for my true personality to shine through. That is how Courtney came into my life.

Before I knew it, I was done with school. I had the option of moving home or I could do what I set out to do, which was move to San Diego. I had met a couple of girls on Craigslist who were in search of a roommate. With the help of my friend, Josh, I packed my gear into my truck and set off for my new home. Before leaving, I spent one last night with Courtney. She wanted to stay with her family in Phoenix. She knew I had to leave the state of Arizona; I felt like a fish out of water there. I was never in love with Courtney, but in the short time I knew her, I knew she could have been someone I could spend a long time with. It was just not the right time in my life, and she wanted to stay in a state I had no desire to return to. She really impacted my life and to this day I still think of her on occasion. So off I went, leaving Phoenix and leaving some good friends I would never forget who truly were there for me in my time of need.

Mira Mesa, a suburb of San Diego, was the location of my new home—15 minutes from Black's Beach in La Jolla. When I left Carrabba's in Phoenix, my boss helped me transfer to another restaurant, Roy's. Instead of searching for work in the diesel mechanic field, I surfed and waited tables. I did not have the confidence to look for jobs in my new field, nor the desire.

Black's Beach was my new surf spot, and it was where I spent most of my time. Parking on a cliff, you would have to hike down the side of a mountain to reach the beach and then walk 15 minutes before arriving at its very localized surf break. Black's is more notable for being a nude beach than a surfing attraction. I witnessed nude volleyball games, sunbathing, good-looking woman and not so good-looking men. I was not fazed, I had surfing back in my life. I remember standing on that cliff for the first time, 300 feet above the manmade trail over-looking the Pacific Ocean, smiling and remembering the feeling I was about to experience. I surfed all day and felt at peace being back in the water.

My job at Roy's was not yet set in stone. My old boss at Carrabba's, Chris, spoke with the manager at Roy's about me, and I was waiting for a phone call. So in the meantime I just surfed and hung out with my new roommates, Jamie and Chris-tina. Both great girls, they introduced me to their friends and took me out to a couple of parties. Even to this day, I feel quite anxious in new environments, with new people. Being 22 years old, from the East Coast, I could not really relate to those I met in San Diego. The culture, upbringing and growing up can be quite different throughout the Country, from State to State. Arizona gave me a very comforting feeling with those who I felt I could be myself around. I never felt that in San Diego. Early on, I chose to spend the time I was not surfing tak-ing Christina's two dogs to Ocean Beach where I felt the most joy and comfort.

When I began working at Roy's, things were even more intense than Carrab-ba's. In order to serve at Roy's, you had to go through all the different stations from pastries to hosting to sushi. I found it challenging to learn about the wines and ingredients in the dishes, while selling to the high-class couples and families dining out in La Jolla. I was expected to know which wine would go best with each meal, and these would change biweekly. This was going up a few levels in the restaurant business, and with the lack of experience, I felt that there was always something new to learn, and frequently something I was missing or forgot. I found a massive difference between the group I had just left in Phoenix and this new one in San Diego. I can only remember two people I felt comfortable talking to at the whole restaurant.

Roy's was in a little plaza just off of Genesee Avenue, roughly 20 minutes from Black's Beach. I would always change on the way to work after my surf; there was always plenty of time due to the horrendous traffic. In Phoenix I would feel excitement on the drive to work, stoked to talk to my friends. In San Diego I felt nervous.

I was not attempting to get work with my new degree; I had no interest really. Work at the restaurant was getting redundant and at times very stressful. Looking back, this was not a mistake, just a learning experience, and a good one. After just a few months in Mira Mesa, California, I made the decision to go back home to Florida. Besides not having steady work and running out of money, I really did not see a successful future there at the time. I was also still young, 22, and I found it hard to make new friends, feeling like I did not quite fit in with the "cool kids" of San Diego.

Back on the road, eastbound for Florida, I felt at ease. Going through Texas, I got a flat tire and had to stay at a really sketchy hotel. I was reminded of an old Alfred Hitchcock movie, *Psycho*. There was a little house behind the hotel I was staying in, and it seemed very similar to the one in the movie... creepy. It was late at night and luckily it happened near an exit. It was a small town and their repair shop opened early the next morning. It was one of those towns that makes you feel like you are in a different world, not the little U.S. beach town I grew up in. The diversity of cultures throughout the U.S. can really blow your mind when you step out of your state and explore. I made the best of the night and got a new tire the next morning. I left the town, happy to make it out alive. Texas was the worst part of the drive by far. I felt like I was in that one state for days. I spoke with my buddy, Rob, almost every day for support throughout my 14 month adventure; Rob and my sister were the only ones who knew I was moving back to Florida. It was just like when I left—I really did not tell many people.

My first glimpse of the Atlantic Ocean was a good one. We just happened to have waves the day I arrived back home. I drove to my parent's house to unload my truck and then I went straight to my buddy Ryan's house for a surf. The water felt amazing, no wetsuit, back to the tropics. I surfed for three and a half hours. I missed the fact that I just left the best waves in the U.S., but I was back where I came from and it felt new again, comfortable. It is a sacrifice, leaving home for something you love. Sometimes it works, sometimes it is just not the right time... but you can always try again.

Once again, I made another restaurant transfer. This time is was Carrabba's in Merritt Island, Florida. Having already gone through the vigorous training at the Phoenix Carrabba's, I was ready. The hiring process was simple, quick personality test, application and then I was told to come back for the menu test. I had the job set up just like that.

Back at home with mom and pops, the feeling was different. I had grown up and learned some important life lessons, moving across the country at 21 years of age. Now I had to adjust to living with the folks again. Nevertheless, I was so stoked to just be able to walk across the street to the beach. I was living very close to the beach in California but with traffic it added an extra half hour just to get to Black's, the closest beach in La Jolla. I also had Smokey and Frances back, and they were so excited to see me. I had missed my dogs so much. They both slept in bed with me for the first week I was home.

Hank was the proprietor of Carrabba's and right from the start he seemed to have it out for me. I never understood why, I just did my job and played by the rules. Once again, I caught on quickly. I won most of the food running contests and some of the sales contests. That was something I liked about this store – the contests. They were good incentive to make sales on certain food and wines. If you won, you would receive a free meal or a drink. Not to mention, the harder you worked waiting tables, the faster the time passed, and usually you would pull in more money. I was killing it in sales, customers liked me and I had a couple cool female friends I worked with who were kind of cute. I was not back in school and had no plans to return.

"Making these rash decisions at a young age can and will sculpt who you grow into. Sometimes we look back at them as being the best decisions we ever make. This was one of them for me. "

Date here this was the trip that changed the direction my life was heading. Rob was traveling to San Diego to train with three-time Mr. Olympia Frank Zane. He extended an offer for me to go with him. A quick trip of four or five days; I could get my shifts covered, no problem.

I met Rob when I was 12 years old, attending Roosevelt Elementary School in Cocoa Beach. He quickly became a part of our little clique, trading baseball cards and skateboarding with us. I had introduced the band Metallica to Rob, which was popular at the time. That was our initial connection - music. Seven years later Rob moved into Sea Oats, the condo building across the street from my house. People change a lot in the span of seven years, as did Rob. He was now heavily tattooed and an expert in music. Hanging with Rob became part of my daily routine. Rob's mother was running a very successful business in North Carolina, which he helped operate. Because the business was operated out of North Carolina, Rob had quite a bit of down time. That down time turned him into a very talented musician with a strong desire to travel around the U.S. He included me in most of his travels throughout our 20s. Looking back, I do believe it was Rob that opened up those initial doors that ultimately gave me the desire to travel around the world.

Sometimes spontaneous trips are the best trips. When I decided to go to Cali with Rob, we were on a plane within hours. We were flying into San Diego. Our plan was to stay at the San Diego Hyatt and visit our high school friend Daniel. Rob would train with Frank, and I would surf.

The waves were good the first day I surfed. I paddled out at Ocean Beach Pier — the conditions were clean and about head high. We were staying right in downtown San Diego area, so it was easy to get around. My favorite little beach community in S.D. was, and still is, Ocean Beach; Interstate 8 dead ends right into it. Ocean Beach had many of the same qualities as Cocoa Beach, a town ruled by locals who were easy to pick out of the crowd just by their appearance and the way they moved. Right on the boardwalk there were skaters, bikers, homeless, all kinds of different people hanging out. Ocean Beach was once known as the Haight-Ashbury of San Diego. You can only imagine some of the characters you come across here.

As planned, Rob met with Frank and I surfed for those first three days. It was no surprise to me that Rob would want to stay. It was while we were having lunch with our friend Danielle that Rob proposed that if I wanted to stay, he could fund our trip up the coast.

All I would have to do was call my co-workers and try to get my shifts covered. I called just about everyone who could possibly help me out. I had no luck and decided it was time to call the boss and explain my situation. The phone call did not go exactly as planned.

I did my best to explain to Hank my opportunity and how I tried to cover my shifts. We did not even discuss options, he went right into telling my I was not a team player and he would have to let me go.

With this unexpected termination, I had the time to travel up the coast of California with my best friend. I never felt good about leaving a job on bad terms, although depending on the job, and your circumstances, sometimes maybe an instant termination or resignation can turn into instant gratification, a real feeling of freedom. I meet many people with jobs where they feel stuck, knowing what their lives have in store. A cut and dry way of life with no real excitement besides that two weeks every year when you are able to have a bit of an adventure. The truth is, the older you get the harder it is to make such a choice, making a sacrifice to maybe start afresh. But great risks can come with great rewards. Making these rash decisions at a young age can and will sculpt who you grow into. Sometimes we look back at them as being the best decisions we ever make. This was one of them for me.

Rob and I continued from San Diego to Los Angeles, San Francisco to Las Vegas. Two weeks of experiencing what some would say, the best the United States has to offer. Nothing too exciting happened on this trip, although for Rob and I, our memories of who we met, the places we stayed and decisions we made, still are the favorite topics of our discussions.

I was returning home, jobless. Although I just experienced one of the best trips of my life, I still needed to make money. Carrabba's was out of the question considering I left the Merritt Island store on bad terms. I had been working with the OSI Corporation for the past few years now. Having worked most of the hotels and restaurants in town, I was almost out of options. I needed something close to my house and worth my time. I had a new outlook on restaurants, considering I was waiting tables and not bussing. You really learn a lot and gain valuable social skills waiting tables. That was one good thing about my move; I came back more confident and eager to see what else the world has to offer.

I skated up to the pier, which sits half a mile from my home on Ocean Beach BLVD. That was my first and only stop for job applications. I got my first job at the Pier at 15. I worked one night in the kitchen as a dishwasher and never came back. I was just a kid and I could not stand washing dishes. Being 22, I had matured and was ready to give it another shot, except this time I had the experience from my time in Arizona, where I came out of my social shell. My interview was a good one. I knew I was hired right off the bat and was told to come back in a few days for training.

The Pier was a great place to wait tables. The dining room overlooks the north side of the pier so you can see the surf, which was both good and bad. When the waves were firing, it was torture having to work and look at everyone out there surfing. If things were slow and the right people were working, it would sometimes be possible to slip out and surf. It usually just took a bribe to the manager. I got along great with all my managers, which was very important. Almost everyone at the Pier were long time Cocoa Beach and Cape Canaveral natives, including Jared, the Cocoa Beach legend. My dad had bartended some of the old bars in the 80s and recognized a lot of the names of bartenders I was now working with 20 years later.

The slow season at the Pier is during winter. Getting through winter can be difficult due to lack of business. This is a time when all the servers are fighting for shifts. Even if you score a shift on a Friday or Saturday night, you may still have only a few tables the whole evening. Once summer hits, it is a whole new ball game. Summertime at the Pier gets very busy. With air shows, boat races and shuttle launches, the Pier gets lots of business. Next thing I knew I was making good money. I was surrounded by good management and friendly co-workers. Some of those co-workers were graduates of Cocoa Beach High School who either attended my year or my sister Kelly's. Growing up in the same town made it really easy to bond with everyone. After a few weeks, I became very satisfied with my job. I did need to find a new career though; I did not want to wait tables for the rest of my life. I needed something with a future and a retirement plan. I had not used my degree in diesel mechanics and was not planning on it. I was still a handful of credits short of my associate degree at Brevard Community College. Even if I had it, I did not know what I wanted to do with it yet. Any kind of schooling is productive, but it is making sure what you are going to school for is something you have interest and skill in.

It was 2007 when I decided to take the first responder class at BCC. One of my buddies at the time worked as a physical therapist and started pushing me toward the medical field. In this day and age, when it comes to career choices, you must make sure jobs will still be available in your chosen field in 20 years. Technology is rapidly taking over, and in some areas jobs are very scarce. I thought maybe working in the medical field was not such a bad idea. This was when the best chapter of my life began.

CHAPTER FIVE

PRACTICING LEADERSHIP

"Before you are a leader, success is all about growing yourself. When you become a leader, success is all about growing others."

—JACK WELCH

The coast has always been my backyard. Growing up, my parents took my sister, Kelly, and me to the beach just about every day. We would get home, play with our dogs Shadow and Light, and usually end up back in the sand before sunset. The ocean was my home away from home right across the street. I had a few friends who started lifeguarding at the time I was still preoccupied with surfing and skating, consumed by the feeling it gave me. I recall one summer when I was extremely close to trying out, but once again I put it off.

Lifeguard tryouts are held every year in late January and March at the Merritt Island High School and consist of completing a 500 meter swim in less than 10 minutes and a 2 mile run in under 20 minutes. The swim is done in a pool and the run is conducted on a track. Tryouts may involve anywhere from 20 applicants to over 100. When there are more applicants than spots available, they will take those with the best times. Upon acceptance you must complete a 40-hour first responder class and then a 60-hour lifeguard academy. The lifeguard academy is grueling. All the new rookie lifeguards sit in a classroom on Saturdays and train on the beach on Sundays. The Saturday classes consist of going through the procedures, drills, rescue/swimming techniques and first aid medical treatment. This is all taught through the Standard Operating Procedures (SOP) manual. The SOPs are split into seven chapters. The chapters cover everything from rules, the merit system and preventative actions to tides, conditions and weather.

Sundays involve intense training where you put what you have learned to use. The rookies are split into two groups called boat crews and they compete against each other, a similar practice is used by the Navy Seals. One of the most important events is the run, swim, run. This event takes place all three Sundays and is timed. You must complete the event in less than 20 minutes. Once completed on time, you must still participate in the other two Sunday events, and either try to beat your best time or just encourage your teammates. Other events consist of tower procedures and the proper sequence of actions to take during a rescue. Not all rookies make the cut.

Passing the initial run and swim does not mean that you are in. If you do not pass the run, swim, run in under 20 minutes, you are out of the academy. The events are meant to train as well as educate. All days involve long distance running and swimming. Once the 60-hour academy is finished, the rookies get their USLA certificate and officially become ocean lifeguards.

Moving back to Florida in 2005 from California was a chance for a new start. I had lost touch with a lot of contacts that I went to high school with. When I left Florida, I failed to tell many of my friends I was leaving. So once I returned, it was like a new town. Now more than ever, I surfed as much as I possibly could. Living in the desert for so long made me want to make up for all that lost time. I now had the beach across the street again and realized how good I have always had it. It took moving across the county to really appreciate what I had, and now I had it back.

So there I was working at the Pier waiting tables and living back at home. In the past year and a half, I had the taste of living with a girl, being on my own and living with roommates. That was my decision when I was in California—move back home and start afresh. Take a deep breath and realize this will take time. I began to go out a bit more often than I used to. Now that I had the Sandbar across the street, I could just walk home and not worry about driving. The Sandbar was a little bar and grill on the beach across from my house. I would also go to a bar called Time Out on Thursday nights. I was going out two to four times a week, which turned into a routine.

Sandbar had to be my favorite bar and I went there more than anywhere else. I started running into my buddy, Jeff, from Merritt Island. Jeff was the captain of his high school swim team—a tall, dark-haired, good-looking guy in good shape. We first met when we were 16 when we used to party at his grandfather's house in Cape Canaveral. That must have been our bonding experience, plus we both loved to surf. I always knew Jeff as "the lifeguard."

Jeff, at the time, was the assistant chief lifeguard of Brevard County. He had been working as an ocean lifeguard since he was 16 and worked his way up the ranks through the years. One night, Jeff suggested I should try out for lifeguarding. The next tryouts were to be held in February of 2008. I figured what better way to make money than sit on the beach, get a tan, meet girls and surf. I was also not doing anything else really, so why not.

December of 2007 was when I met a girl that impacted me for the rest of my life, Lindsay. I was with my normal crew of buddies when we went to Time Out on Thursday night. It was halfway through the night when a fight almost broke out at the bar. This absolutely beautiful girl looked at me and asked in a sarcastic tone, "Where am I?" That was our icebreaker that led to a conversation about where we were from and what brought us both to that moment in life. She liked my tattoos and I liked her style, there was an instant mutual attraction. She was wearing blue jeans with an elegant white top, having just finished a modeling shoot. Unlike most of the girls in the bar, she was dressed very classy. I did not tell Devin or Jeff that I had met this girl. It was more of a brief encounter.

I went about the rest of my night, had a couple of drinks and decided to leave. Time Out Sports Bar is on the second floor of a hotel. At the end of each night, everyone congregates downstairs in front of the entrance. As I was in the crowd, I spotted Lindsay talking with a friend. I patiently waited for them to break away. I walked up to her to say goodnight. She smiled as soon as she saw me approaching her. I noticed her green eyes right away and her giant beautiful smile. She looked even better in the outside light - about 5'5" and very petite with long, wavy dirty blonde hair and long eyelashes. I got her number and felt I had met someone truly special that night, just a normal Thursday night at Time Out.

The following day, Jeff, Devin and myself all paddled out for a surf in front of the Piñata Causeway. It was a cold December morning. I had just met an amazing girl and was about to surf hollow Florida waves, both rarities in Cocoa Beach. This turned out to be one of the best Florida days I had ever surfed considering where my head was at the time, a feeling of love mixed with the rhythm of surfing.

Late December 2007 was getting colder. It was starting to feel much more like the holiday season. I was working at the pier up in the restaurant and vividly remember walking to the outside deck overlooking the south side of the coastline. The waves were small and the weather was chilly. I gave Lindsay a call for the first time, and we made an arrangement to meet up.

Later that night Lindsay met me at my dad's house once I got off work. We were having our Christmas party at work that night, and I came home right after our little gift exchange. I was anxious to beat her there, so I could get cleaned up and shower. I had a couple friends, Mike and Melanie, who showed up at my house just before Lindsay was meant to arrive. I did not want to be rude, so I just entertained my guests until she got there. Once she did, my friends quickly got the hint and took off. As we were talking, I learned that she surfed. Not only that, but she also was a musician. We shared the same passion for music; that's very rare for me to find. We did not go anywhere; we just sat in my kitchen and talked for a couple of hours.

We met back up that following Thursday night at Time Out, played some pool and had a couple of drinks. She told me all about her family history and her childhood in Panama City. She was not like any other girl I had ever met. She was always making me laugh with her sarcasm and wit. I found her to be by far the prettiest girl I had ever laid my eyes on. Not to mention she had all the qualities I liked. We sat in her car and talked for what seemed like ages, just about our lives and what we have done and what we would like to do. Denny's is directly next door to Time Out, so we decided to get some late night breakfast. I carried her across the wooded area between the bar and Denny's on my back to keep her feet dry. We ordered breakfast and continued talking into the early morning. That was our first official date and that was when I knew I had met someone very special.

Just a few days later we went surfing together for the first time. It was a chest high day at the Cocoa Beach Pier with clean, fun conditions. After we both got acclimated to the conditions and cool water, we began mentally critiquing each other's surfing abilities. I was impressed with her surfing skills. We got back to my house and had some lunch. I had to go to work in a couple of hours so we were just hanging out. As I was getting my work clothes out of the dryer, Lindsay punched me in the arm after I made a comment about her surfing. We both started laughing and that is when I kissed her. Up until this point, I think we were both trying to figure out how the other one felt, gauging one another's feelings. She had many guy friends, considering she was in a mostly male-dominated sport, at least at that time it was. So I was trying to watch her mannerisms and how she acted around me to see if my feeling was mutual. After kissing her, I knew it definitely was. Lindsay was all I could think about. We began texting on a frequent basis. She was living in Satellite Beach but was making regular trips home to Panama City. At the time I was living in Cocoa Beach.

February of 2008 was the month I tried out for lifeguarding. The meeting point was Merritt Island High School pool at 6 a.m. The weather was chilly, somewhere around 60 degrees. The drill was to swim 500 meters in under 10 minutes. I did not consider surfing to be much different to swimming. The pool was the epicenter for lifeguards. Once I arrived, I spotted Jeff right away. He was standing next to the chief, Wyatt. This was the first time I met Wyatt, although he was a popular guy around Cocoa Beach. He was known for his paddleboarding records and his numerous years with Ocean Rescue. My first impression of him was that he was strictly business. I did not really get to speak with Wyatt due to all the activity going on around us. One of the captains present was Troy. Troy was a Merritt Island born and raised fisherman. He was all about boats, dirt bikes, fishing and surfing. He held all the qualities of a great lifeguard. He spent three years on the swim team, and was going into his sixth season of lifeguarding. Iain was another captain who was there. Iain was Troy's best friend and seemed to be very stern when I met him. I could tell that he was a competitor, and a skilled, seasoned lifeguard. There were a few other lifeguards helping out and taking times. I hopped in the pool and got ready for my swim. When Wyatt blew the whistle, I was off. My swimming techniques were amateurish. I am not sure how I managed to swim the set distance under 10 minutes, but I did. I swam the whole 500 meters with my head above water. Wyatt looked at Jeff and said, "This is your boy?"

My run was much better than my swim. I had passed the swim in just over nine minutes and my two-mile run was around 14 minutes. I had made the cut along with 19 other rookies. I figured the hard part was over. I did not realize that the lifeguard academy would be so brutal and challenging.

First day in the classroom was very educational. Wyatt told many stories and taught us the fundamentals of lifeguarding. One thing he said to the class that I will never forget was: "From here on out, you will never look at the beach the same way you did before lifeguarding." He was right. From here on out, the beach would become an office, not just the playground it had been my whole life. The training classroom was located at the fire rescue center just over the bridge from Merritt Island to Rockledge. Saturdays would involve classroom sessions from 8 a.m. to 4 p.m. for three consecutive weekends. There would be a lot of information to absorb, but it was all very interesting, which made it easy to retain.

The first Sunday was absolute torture. Wyatt's training seemed more like a boot camp for marines. He had us running and swimming constantly with little breaks for water. I managed to strain my knee at one point but just hobbled along and finished each event. If we were not running, we were swimming. Aside the physical events, we also practiced with emergency situations and scenarios. The next day, I found it hard to walk, as expected. Jeff warned me that Wyatt's training techniques were hard core. I knew what to expect for the next two Sundays.

The following Saturday we watched multiple rescue videos. Huntington Beach has a series of training videos that are used in each rookie class, which were quite helpful. The next day was much like the first Sunday with lots of running and swimming. One event, the chain run, was intense. We all took turns jumping off the jetty pier. Once everyone had entered the water, we all linked up with our rescue cans and swam around the jetty as a team. The drill was not to break the chain and also to get the feeling of rescuing a victim and experiencing the weight of swimming them to shore. Once on shore, we ran around two miles, still all attached. This was a cool event, keeping us all together as a team. We ran some more medical scenarios and that constituted most of our second Sunday.

The last classroom day was shorter than the others considering it was our last class day. Wyatt took a lot of this time to speak to us about the fundamentals of lifeguarding and the importance of watching the water. Between Jeff and Wyatt, there were many different stories and scenarios to learn from. The last Sunday was brutal. Besides all the normal drills, run, swim, run, and beach flags, we did the gauntlet.

The gauntlet was done by every rookie class but had never been completed. The event involved running from the jetty to the Cocoa Beach Pier. While running we had to carry a paddleboard above our heads, all trying to keep pace. Once we reached the pier, we had to enter the water and swim back as a team. The distance from the jetty to the pier is three and a half miles. We all took turns during the run to share the task of carrying the paddleboard. Once we reached the pier, we were spent, but now it was time to swim. Considering we had three and a half miles to paddle and swim, we all had to keep each other motivated and pumped up. We would take turns on the paddleboard, like we did during the run. Constantly changing paddleboarders was good for keeping us relatively warm. We had a chance to be out of the water and under the sun. It seemed like eternity, but roughly two and a half hours later, we were closing in. By the time we reached the jetty, four rookies had to swim in, exhausted. We were the first rookie class to complete the gauntlet, and we all made the cut as USLA certified Ocean Rescue lifeguards.

My first day on the job was at the pier. I was working with a lieutenant named Jason. Jason was a good guard to work with for the first day. He had a very sarcastic sense of humor, which matched well with mine. He showed me the ropes and told me all the right things to get in the habit of doing. We set up perimeter flags around the tower, and he showed me the correct set up of the tower gear. I spent most of the time blowing the whistle to keep swimmers from drifting into the pier. A few times I thought I may have to enter the water, but never had too. The day just flew by. It was just how I imagined, a day at the beach.

I was the low man on the totem pole so I worked slow towers for the most part. I soon began to befriend the captains, and I began working busier towers. I was using a theory known as leader - member exchange. The exchange conceptualizes leadership as a process that is centered on the interactions between leaders and followers. Your personality, along with other characteristics, are a huge part of this process. Becoming a part of the 'in-group' allows you to become a part of the decision making process, thus, making you a valuable asset. I did not know I was using this theory back then, although now looking into these different practices I see just how well they can actually work. Nevertheless, the authenticity of the individual is imperative in this process, otherwise it can be quite obvious that you are just looking to climb the corporate ladder. In my case, I befriended those captains and they became some of my best friends even outside work.

I distinctly remember the first time I surfed at work. I was working with my friend, Kevin, who does not surf, at the slowest tower in the county. The waves were waist high with glassy conditions – basically your typical summer Florida day when things are good. I managed to get a couple of fun waves and thoroughly enjoyed my day working my dream job. As the summer went on, we had a few rescues but nothing too serious. I worked mainly in the north end of the county considering that was where the crowds were.

Around six months into my first year, I was promoted to captain. All tower guards wear red shorts. The officers in charge all wear blue shorts. I was six months into my rookie year and was in blue shorts. There were a few lifeguards who were a bit irritated that I was promoted so fast. Most of the lifeguards in Brevard County are young kids; for the most part, high schoolers. I was the oldest rookie in my class at 24. I had age on my side, and it also helped that I showed up early everyday and sometimes even on my days off. I wanted to work, and I did. All you had to do was show up and you were put to work most of the time. Every day typically at least one of the six zones is short on lifeguards, mostly teenage no shows. Everyone knew to call me if they were short and I would come in. When you work all the time, you get to know everyone. I knew everyone pretty well. That is how I could tell by people's reactions and mannerisms how they felt about me being in charge of them. Although I was liked, I did my job and held quite a few traits required of a leader. I had the intelligence needed for working on the beach, having over 20 years experience of dipping my feet in the sand on that very same shoreline. I had also picked up very good social skills from my time in the restaurant business, which also gave me more confidence. There are some valuable skills you must learn in order to lead well. These include being social, as there is an art to speaking as well as an art to getting people to listen.

I started running Zone 6, Spessard Holland in Melbourne Beach, which is roughly 25 miles from Cocoa Beach. I had the feeling that no one really respected me as a captain. I was still a rookie, so I could see why they would hold a grudge. I cannot say I would respect someone jumping in a supervisor position during their first year on the job unless they had a lot of training and experience on their resume. I just had to work to the best of my abilities and try to be a good leader. The south beaches were mostly full of locals. All the tourists in the county were hanging out at Ron Jon's and at the closest beach, Sheppard Park.

Overall, my first year was a good one. I spent the rest of the year in charge of Zone 6. As time went on, I got to know all the south guards. Bonds were made; working with someone for eight hours, you will get to know him whether you like it or not. I had moved to Satellite Beach to get away from my hometown for a while. I did miss the busy beaches in the north. On occasion I would still work in the north, usually on a day off if I could get overtime and they were short on guards. Jeff had made a good call having me start off working in the south, so I could develop relationships, gain experience and ease into my new role.

Wyatt and Jeff had been trying for years to gain full time, year-round service with Ocean Rescue. For years they were unsuccessful. In 2007, Central Florida had 10 drownings due to rip currents along Brevard County beaches. *Forbes* magazine labeled our beach the fourth most deadly in the world that year. During Memorial Day weekend there were over 200 rescues. I remember the day vividly. I walked across the street to go surfing and my buddy Garrett was sitting tower at Sheppard Park, rescue after rescue all day. This was a treacherous weekend on the Central Florida coastline.

It was a summer day when Jeff approached me with a huge grin on his face. "Bro, you are never going to believe this!" He proceeded to tell me that Ocean Rescue was granted full time year-round coverage. The news got even better when he told me I was one of the nine full time captains.

This was some of the best news I had received in a long time. So the deal was that all the full time lifeguards had to become EMTs. The county paid for seven of the nine full timers to get their EMT certificate. The other two were already certified. Meanwhile, the whole organization was about to experience a radical shift. I had entered the Ocean Rescue organization just in time.

Ocean Rescue's summer season ends at the beginning of August once high school is back in session. I now was not only lifeguarding in the summer time but in the heart of winter too. After the 10 drownings of 2007, the county decided to budget for more towers - 13 were not enough. Now during the summer, we would have 26 towers open along the beaches of Brevard County. Year-round we would have five operational towers. There are towers at the pier, Sheppard Park, Lori Wilson Park, Coconuts and down south on Paradise Beach. So in the summer time with a fully staffed beach, there were 46 lifeguards on duty each day. In the winter time with a fully staffed beach, there were nine guards on duty each day. All nine of us were now full time county employees with a retirement plan and benefits.

Working on the beach in winter time can get lonely. I really got to know all the guards that first winter of 2008. We did not really have much of a choice but to get to know each other, with the days getting longer and longer as the winter wore on. Troy and Iain were full timers, along with Scott who was next in rank.

Scott had been lifeguarding for around five seasons and worked primarily in Zone 2. I took a liking to Scott. I would not trust him around my girlfriend if I had one, but I liked the guy. We both absolutely loved girls so we would talk about them all day long. My days went by fast, working with Scott. Along with Iain and Troy, these three were the leaders of the pack, under the supervision of Wyatt and Jeff. With time and experience they all put in, they all knew what to do in most emergency situations, and were looked and relied upon to act and lead. They were all captains in the north, the busiest beaches in the county.

Justin, another long time lifeguard, was primarily down south and still is to this day. He is the nicest person I have ever met. Justin was a family man with a great wife and a bundle of children. He took his job seriously and always competed in lifeguard competitions to represent our country. He was by far the fittest lifeguard we had—he was roughly six foot tall with long wavy blond hair and absolutely shredded. Justin was a motivator, always positive and always showing gratitude towards each and every one of us through all of the years that followed.

Grant had been with Ocean Rescue for a few years prior to going full time. He was also one of the original nine captains. Grant was in Scott's rookie class and was one of the most experienced lifeguards we had, although he slipped quite a few times in the later years, which ultimately got him terminated. Rachel was our only full time female captain. Rachel had two young boys, both of whom loved the beach and had long blond hair. She came to lifeguard with us from Pompano Beach in South Florida. With her prior experience in a full time organization, Jeff and Wyatt made a choice to have her onboard.

Brett was also a rookie when hired on, like myself. Brett was a hunter/fisherman raised out in West Melbourne who already held EMT certification. Brett was a good old boy and held many similarities with the Fire Chief and many firefighters of Brevard County; he became one of them in the years to come. Brett would later end up running a zone in the south.

Johnny, another rookie, was also hired on full time, like me, due to his age and being a lifelong surfer from Melbourne Beach. Johnny was a great surfer and good company. Like Justin, Johnny was one of our best trainers for the rookies and upcoming leaders. He was trustworthy and had a special skill when it came to influencing others. Johnny was in the rookie class that ran right after mine. He spent the last couple of years managing Da Kine Diego's in Satellite Beach. Da Kine's is the all time best little surfer burrito place in Central Florida.

The food was great but the lifeguarding was a much better gig. The nine of us were all set up with what we referred to as dream jobs.

The job changed drastically with the seasons. Not having to manage 100 seasonal lifeguards gave the job more of a cruisy beach feel. Not to mention that some days went by without a single person on the beach. But there are lots of winter days with patrons still on the beach, so it was important to have lifeguards. One of my most memorable rescues was during the time of year that lifeguards were not usually on duty. I was working at Lori Wilson Park with Troy.

A rip current started to form just north of the tower. Troy and I both noticed it. The beach was not packed that day, but still there was a small crowd. Right when we noticed the rip, a couple drifted into it. I sprinted 100 yards or so to the water's edge and swam out to make contact. The couple was not that far from shore, which made it easy to reach them. They grabbed the can and I swam them in. Once I made it to the shore I started jogging back to the tower. Just then I heard yelling from the water. I turned to see a little girl and her father caught in a flash rip just a few meters to the south. I sprinted back to the water and started to swim. I swam with my head above water to keep my eyes on the girl and her dad. I had not seen panic in someone's eyes until then. The young girl was wearing a mask and snorkel, and her mask was all fogged up and she was screaming for help. Her father was right behind her, just trying to stay above water. There was an empty gaze in his eyes and a sheer look of terror. He was a heavy-set man and was clearly in need of rescue. I reached the two quickly and swam them to shore. I had to go in a couple more times that day, but not for anything as serious as the man and his little girl. A couple of hours later, the family was leaving the beach and stopped at my tower to thank me again. That meant so much to me; saving someone's life gave me this overwhelming feeling of purpose. From that day forward, I realized that preventing these rescues from ever happening would make me the best at what I do, moreso, to teach these preventative techniques to teenagers would be the biggest challenge as a captain.

Full time season at the beach ends at the beginning of August, with all towers open only on weekends until the end of October. So it was now October, and even though it was just weekends for 26 towers, during the week the full timers were still on the beach staffing the five towers.

There was a change in November of 2008. Our Ocean Rescue chief, Wyatt, resigned from his position to pursue his career in the Coast Guard and Brevard

County Fire Rescue. This was an unexpected loss. When Wyatt resigned, Jeff took over the role as an interim chief. I knew that Jeff would be our official chief in the months to come. He carried all the traits of a leader. His intelligence in the medical field and waterman skills placed him above the rest in our organization. Leaders can develop their abilities through experience, practice and instructions, and there is no doubt that Jeff attained them throughout his 10 years at the organization.

The new interim assistant chief was not made official either. One of our captains in the north, Eisen, had been with Ocean Rescue for seven seasons and it was thought by most of us that he would get the position. He held the skill set of a great manager moreso than a leader. Both Jeff and Eisen would have to sit in front of the fire chief, district chief, basically all the bigwigs for an interview. Jeff was much liked by all of them. The chiefs of Brevard County are big hunters and fishermen. I would not say they were watermen like Wyatt. Jeff had all the qualities they found fit for the role.

Jeff was raised in Merritt Island, and grew up fishing, hunting and surfing. He was also going on his 10th year with Ocean Rescue. He was currently taking classes as a part of his engineering degree, which he kept working on over the years. He was basically a shoo-in, as everyone knew Jeff and respected him. Eisen only had competition from two other lifeguards and a couple of outsiders who were in with the county at one time or another. Both Jeff and Eisen ultimately got the positions.

The only very noticeable change at first had to do with Jeff being a very nice, laid-back individual. Wyatt, on the other hand, was an ex-Navy diver who was constantly yelling and barking orders. If Wyatt were to pull up to tower and you were not doing what you were supposed to be doing, he would tear you apart. Wyatt was a great lifeguard, probably the best I have ever known in many regards, but not the best leader or manager. Jeff was well known by all the lifeguards and was a great leader and manager, but the guy who everyone was scared of was now gone. We went from having a leader with coercive power to one with referent power.

Ideally, the full time captains and lieutenants would hold similar leadership traits that could be passed down to the seasonal lifeguards each summer. It took some time adjusting to the change in ranks, along with the new hours and SOPs, but we all worked as a team and got the job done.

December was starting to get cold, but there were still lots of people on the beach. This was the time to go through all the medical supplies, see what we needed and prepare for the summer. For the most part, we were slow in the winter time. We were the last county in Florida to go full time with our Ocean Rescue program. I always found that strange as we are the Space Coast, generating a lot of tourism in Florida, even during the winter. Not to have full time protection on the beach was dangerous. Well, now we had it.

I had spent the summer working the southernmost portion of the beach, which was also the slowest. Then the following summer, I was working at the pier in north Brevard. This worked out very well for me, since I worked at the Pier House Restaurant four nights a week. As soon as my day of lifeguarding on the beach was over, I would change into my Pier uniform. I wore black pants, long sleeve white button down, a green apron and black shoes. It was a funny switch from a pair of lifeguard baggies to a penguin suit.

I really got to know Iain and Troy since I was working in Zone 1 most of the time. Iain was one of the most conditioned lifeguards we had on the beach. Every morning he would either run or swim. He had been lifeguarding a total of six seasons and had performed CPR numerous times. Troy was Iain's partner in crime. They started lifeguarding together when they were 16, and they usually worked together during winters. These two seemed inseparable and they worked well together. Troy was a little less outgoing and a bit more mellow than Iain. I enjoyed working with the two of them. I felt that I could learn a lot from them, considering they had already put in the time.

I was shifted around in the winter months to work Zone 2 a lot as well as Zone 5 down south. Each zone has its officer or officers in charge during the summer season. In the winter time, it was still the captains' territory. In Zone 1, those leaders were Iain and Troy. The Zone 2 officer in charge was Scott. I had spent many days working with Scott during the winter, more so than anyone else. Scott was the stereotypical lifeguard; he was in good shape and hit on most girls that came to our beaches. He was also someone I referred to as an "old schooler." He had also been with the county five seasons and had a couple CPR stories. We always got along and worked well together.

The officers in charge of Zone 5 were Justin and Rachel. Rachel was very by-the-book and made sure everything was where it should be. At least once a week, she would go through all the equipment and rearrange everything. It drove me crazy but it served a purpose.

Things were always a little confusing coming from the north to Zone 5. Everything almost seemed backwards, but not in a bad way. This just got me in the habit of checking all the equipment every morning so that every tool was accounted for, an essential habit to build in the medical field.

Working in Zone 5 made for a nice change. Paradise Beach is a beautiful beach park with lots of locals and great surf when the right swells come in. When working in the north, you have the option to roam to neighboring towers. In the south, only one tower is staffed in the winter months so there was no roaming around in the ATV unless there was a call from EMS regarding an emergency close enough for us to respond first.

I would bounce around in the winter time, working where I was needed. This was nice because the zone I was running at the end of the summer was not included in our year-round coverage. So now I was getting to know how different officers kept their stations, and how they worked and lead. I liked working in the south due to it being so close to my house in Satellite, but I liked working in the north in Cocoa Beach because it was busy. I acted as a floater for most of the winter, which was fine with me.

It was around this time when we had a group of firefighters come out to the beach and work with us when we needed them. It was very difficult to have nine lifeguards staffing five towers 40 hours a week. This was valuable considering some of the firefighters were paramedics and had been working in EMS for a number of years. We would have eight hours to pick their brains, and learn as much as we could from them. It was also nice to have new faces to work with in the winter months. We all got along great with the small crew of firefighters who worked as part time lifeguards. This only went on for a few months before the county decided to staff us with six permanent part time employees. This was a tremendous help in keeping all the towers staffed and cut down on overtime for the full time guards. There was a period of time when Iain and I worked over two week's straight to rack in the OT. It became very natural for me; I just went to the beach every day, I liked it and I was making good money.

It was during winters that we prepared for the upcoming summer months, and made any adjustments we saw fit. This would be our first year as a full time organization. This would also be Jeff's first year as chief. We received all new medical and tower supplies, which we stocked and organized. A new Zone 1 station was put in at Cherie Down Park, and the station at the pier was moved to Fire Station 61 by Coconuts for the Zone 3 station. This would be my new summer zone. During one of our captain meetings, Jeff asked us all which zone we would like to run in the summertime. Of course, Iain and Troy said Zone 1, a request that would be granted considering they had run it the past six summers. Scott requested Zone 2 and was granted it. Justin and Rachel live down south and had always worked at Paradise, so that was their zone. Brett was going to take Zone 6 in the southernmost part of the county. Johnny and myself would be the captains of Zone 3 on Coconuts Beach.

As the Summer came to an end, we started getting winter gear to keep us warm and make us all uniformed. We received jackets, sweatshirts, sweatpants and beanies. We went through our first winter having to wear our own gear to stay warm. We were also given class B dress attire. Class Bs were to be worn at award ceremonies and all other formal events. As the budget changed, we became more professional, which made us feel more appreciated. This gave us all motivation in one way or another.

Our next rookie tryout, I was assigned to take swim times. Being one of the full time captains gave me the opportunity to get involved with the training. I was also right in the middle of the EMT school with Justin, Scott and Iain. Between full time work and school with clinicals, we were all very busy. This was giving me just what I needed before summer began - experience. Being in charge of a zone in the north, I was guaranteed to have my work cut out for me.

Spring break seemed to roll around quickly. Before we knew it the season had begun. My zone's meeting spot was right at Station 61 behind Coconuts. The station had an overhang for the ambulance and right next to that was all of our tower equipment. We did not have a station for Zone 3, just an area to neatly stack the gear and a couple large storage boxes. The Zone 1 station ended up being placed at Lori Wilson and used as a supply shed. Plus, I did not think the fire station wanted an old tin shed eyesore right next to their fire department. Not many guards were to report to Station 61. As long as we were fully staffed in Zone 3, I had five guards in my area, three at Coconuts and two at 16th Street. I would assign towers first thing and then have all the guards go through their gear to make sure it was all there and accounted for. Considering our location, we would not have enough time to do any PT on the beach before 10 a.m., which was when we needed to be at the tower to open up. So I would use this time to go over medical scenarios.

I was now in my second session and working in south Cocoa Beach. Zone 3 was a brand new zone, and I was going to be the first to run it. This was a great feeling, as I did not feel I was taking someone else's earned station. Spring break was busy, but no real emergencies went down in my assigned area. Coconuts was more about crowd control than anything else, especially on Sundays. Coconuts on Sundays was, and still is, a zoo. For some reason, Sunday is synonymous with fun day in the eyes of all the college kids of Orlando. This is the day they all come to the beach and get drunk, as well as trash the area. Lots of fights break out and tops come off. It really is a great beach for people watching and if you want to meet some drunk college girls, it is the place to be.

When I needed a break from Club Coconuts, I would drive down to 16th Street. I grew up surfing Fourth Street South, so I would usually pass locals and old school mates that I grew up with hanging on the streets. Early April, I was driving to Tower 14 at 16th Street when I came across an old friend of mine I had not seen in ages. Heather was the sister of my high school girlfriend, Morgan. I dated Morgan for two years and would always be at her house with her brothers and sisters. I think I ate dinner at her house more than I did at my own house during those last years of high school. I became really close to Morgan and her family in high school, so when we broke up, it was more than just losing her, but losing her whole family. Heather was on the beach with her husband and little girl. We spoke about her family and Morgan, and reminisced about the days we used to hang out at her house. I told her about my job and how much it meant to me. It seemed like only yesterday I was helping her mom cook dinner.

After catching up, I moved on, and just a few streets further south, I ran into my friend Crystal. Crystal was a manager at a gym in Cocoa Beach. She just came in from a little surf and was playing with her daughter, Emi, in the sand. Once again, a high school friend I had not seen forever. I told her it was my second year lifeguarding, and I was currently looking after a section of Cocoa Beach. It was wild how many people I would run into just driving a couple of miles down the beach. This was just the beginning of what looked like was going to be a great summer.

CHAPTER SIX

3,500

> "I had snapshots of life flickering before my eyes while spinning even faster at a terrifyingly low altitude. I am not entirely sure if I were conscious for the final seconds before hitting the ground or if I lost consciousness due to centrifugal force. Sometimes your brain erases any memory of traumatic events; either way I do not recall the final moments of my plummet to the earth."

During the eight years I had been skydiving, I had always tried to get my family and friends to go. I have had a handful of friends take part in doing tandems, but never family. I never would have guessed that my mom would even think of going skydiving. That is why I was so surprised to receive an email from her saying she and her best friend Linda would be doing tandems just days before my birthday. Linda sent my mom an email in early April, confirming their plan.

> Jane,
>
> I have booked us for Saturday, April 11 at 10 a.m. ... we can bring our own cameras... of course, we cannot jump with them, we have to give them to the staff on the plane and they will be returned after the jump. Spoke to Kathleen who states that the video can include two people except for the jump part... of course during the jump they can only follow one of

> us... I am happy for that to be you as long as we get pics of us together.
>
> Linda

April was going to be a very busy month for me. I was right in the middle of finishing my EMT clinicals. I had to have a clinical on my birthday, April 16, due to my hectic work schedule. I was also going to a show the night before mom's jump day to see the Riverboat Gamblers. Everything was going really well at the time; work was good, I was moving right along with school, and I had a girl who meant more than anything to me.

I was working at the beach at Coconuts on Thursday April 8th, a couple of days before the jump. It was a beautiful day at the beach with perfect weather but the waves were flat, which was no surprise. It was not packed, but there was a decent crowd that day. Once summer began, Coconuts always had something going on to draw a crowd. I could not stop thinking about the jump day. I told all my buddies at work about it. Today would be my last day on the beach until Sunday. For the most part, the day was just like any other.

April 9, I spent doing my clinical at Station 82 with my EMT instructor, Pat. Pat was a great instructor so I knew the day would go well and I would actually learn something. Sometimes when you are a student doing a ride along at a station, it seems like the medics do not want you there. Luckily, I had a couple of guys who were cool with showing me around and actually teaching me what I needed to know. I could always understand why they did not want students. The schedule of a firefighter in Brevard County is 24 hours on and 48 hours off. When a medic is working, his station is like his home for that period of time. So I came to the conclusion, I would not like having to deal with students every single day I worked either. But, on the other hand, the students are the future EMTs and medics, so it is good to make sure they are on top of their game considering they will possibly be saving your life one day.

We only had a couple of calls that day. Our first call was to a diabetic emergency, the more serious of the two. We followed all procedures and transported the patient to the Cape Canaveral Hospital. All and all a normal day for Station 61.

April 10, I had tickets to see the Riverboat Gamblers from Denton, Texas. Garrett was going to accompany me to the show that night. The venue was The Social in downtown Orlando, one of my favorite venues. It is located on Orange Avenue, the main strip downtown, and neighborhood filled with various bars and clubs. I had seen dozens of shows here, most of them with Garrett.

So we made the drive to Orlando and as always, we were running late. Parking downtown is always difficult. This was a weekend night, making things that much worse. We ended up parking in one of the parking garages and ran to The Social. We were so late this time, we actually missed the show. The night was a short one for me, considering I had to be up early and home was an hour away. Since we missed the show, it was looking like Garrett would be spending his evening bar hopping with his college buddies. I said my goodbyes to Garrett and headed back to Satellite.

The morning of April 11, 2009, started like most others, alarm sounded at 8 a.m., and shortly later I was up and ready for the day. This was a special day though; my mom was jumping out of an airplane. I was meeting her at Lily's, a local breakfast café right next door to my tattoo shop in Satellite Beach where we would usually meet once a week to drink coffee and catch up on our lives.

We had a 45-minute drive to get to Skydive Sebastian. I do not recall our conversation or nerves on the drive, if any. Much like my first drive to Skydive Sebastian when I was 18, I imagine my mom had some of those same emotions.

Linda had a crew with her when she arrived. Everyone who was there to watch my mom and Linda were either family or co-workers.

Weekends at Skydive Sebastian were crowded with lots of tandem jumpers. Sebastian is a very popular drop zone, one of the best actually. At least once a month, a skydive boogie was held there; where most of the skydivers went big. They all worked very hard, and played even harder. Due to all the events and formations held at Sebastian, they were always featured in the monthly magazine, *Parachutist*. I have always been proud that this is my home drop zone.

We arrived early, so I decided to do a jump before my mom and Linda's load went up. I also had planned to do my second ever night jump later. Night jumps are always offered when there is a full moon. I had experienced one night jump with Garrett and Jonah a couple years prior. It was quite an intense ride. We had glow sticks and strobe lights mounted on us so we were visible to other jumpers. Cars were parked on the field with their headlights turned on so the landing area was visible. The whole ocean was lit up, with a full moon gleaming down along the Central Florida coastline. It was very memorable and I wanted to experience it again. Jonah was my other jump buddy; he had been a Marine with Garrett when we were all 18. Garret and Jonah got certified after they served their time in the military. They both chose to pack their own parachutes, unlike me. I knew how to pack; I just had rather someone else do it since I only jumped periodically.

The plane was completely full for my first jump of the day. This was typical due to it being a Saturday. This was why I would always go and jump on weekdays; I loved empty airplanes. Once I got comfortable skydiving, while in the plane flying up to altitude I would do a lot of thinking... at a time I should have been visualizing. Going over emergency procedures and the skydive is crucial, no matter your level of experience.

When the plane takes off, everyone must have their helmets and seat belts on, and at 1,500 feet they can come off. If the plane has to make an emergency landing before 2,000 feet, all the jumpers land with the plane. If there is a problem above 2,000 feet, all the jumpers must bail from the plane and use their reserve canopies.

The plane took off and we started climbing to altitude. The more packed the plane, the longer it takes to get to 13,500 feet, which is the usual exit point. The plane took off facing east, so we flew right over the Sebastian Inlet—bright shades of blue ocean with a crystal clear coastline. Depending on wind direction, we would fly east and then do a big circle until we hit the jump run where the plane stalled over the drop zone and the green light came on for the jumpers to exit. Again, depending on the wind direction, we would have any-where from five to 15 second delay between jumpers. This allowed each group, or solo flyer, to have plenty of space in the sky.

We reached altitude and I was one of the jumpers doing a solo free fly, meaning I would be one of the first ones out of the plane. There is belly flying and there is free flying. When belly flying, you are falling approximately 120 miles an hour. While free flying, you reach speeds of up to 200 an hour. Since free flyers reach pulling altitude first, they are normally the first ones out of the plane.

Once I was up, I made my way to the door. The temperature is always cool, even on summer days. With a five second delay, I decided to exit right into a sit fly. My exit was good; as planned I was sit flying the whole jump. Still in the process of mastering this technique, I got a big hit of adrenaline reaching high speeds. At 6,000 feet, I went from sit fly to belly. You always want to be on your belly when you pull your pilot chute, no matter what. I like to face east when I pull, facing the ocean and the inlet. I have always done so since my AFF.

My opening was clean; I had a square, stable and steerable canopy. I had not yet taken a canopy control class, so I did not get too wild under my parachute. The free fall is very fast and gets the adrenaline going. For me, the canopy ride down is the most relaxing part of a skydive. After a while though, everyone wants to get a little more radical, and this is why low turns are the number one cause of fatalities in skydiving. Overall my canopy ride went very well, as I flew my wind pattern took me right to the landing area where I landed softly on my feet.

I instantly saw my mom and her friends, with big smiles on their faces. Just the energy on the field during those moments gave both my mom and Linda an understanding of why this was one of my pastimes. Our load was on deck so it was time for us all to get ready. My rig was being packed, and my mom and Linda were met by their tandem instructors.

Dave was taking my mom and Uwe was taking Linda. Eight years earlier Uwe took me on my first skydive; I remember it well. Dave was one of the nicest guys I have ever met at Sebastian, and I was very happy to have him taking my mom up. Linda was getting video and Craig was shooting. I had told my mom and Linda that once I got to the ground, I would run to the hanger and get the camera to get shots of them landing. I love the expressions on the faces of anyone who jumps for the first time. It is always smiles all around and most of the time the jumpers are speechless. But more notably, it is about sharing that special feeling with them once they made their final approach and landing. It is really in those final moments that they understand why we do such a thing.

For a tandem skydive, there is a quick 10 minute briefing. You get into your harness, and the instructor tells you to keep your head back and arms crossed on exit. Once you exit the plane, the instructor taps your arm and you let both arms go as if you were flying. As far as your legs, you just kick them back. When it is time to land, the instructor has you lift your legs up and he takes the impact. The canopies that are flown for tandems are large enough for two people and allow you to land very softly.

We were off to the loading area. My mom did not seem nervous at all, nor did Linda. That, of course, calmed my nerves. They had a pact that if either one of them decided at the last minute that they did not want to go through with the jump, that would be fine. I was a bit nervous for my mom, not for me. Even though she and Linda had the best of the best of instructors, there was still a chance for something to go wrong. As we approached the plane, Rick, Linda's husband, took a quick photo of my mom and me as we were about to board the plane.

We all loaded the plane in order of groups: tandems, belly flyers and then free flyers. It worked out that I could sit by my mom for the ride to altitude. I do not remember where my head was on that 20-minute ride. I imagine that I was doing my best to visualize my emergency procedures... but in all honestly I cannot be too sure. The only thing I really remember was that they were playing music in the plane. In all the years I have been jumping at Sebastian, I have never once heard them play music on board. It was only until takeoff, then it was turned off. Since then I had never heard them play music again.

Linda was the only one getting video, so there was only one camera guy filming. He knew that the three of us were together, so he managed to get shots of all of us on the way up. Seat belts off at 1,500 feet—we were now in flight.

The climb to altitude took approximately 20 minutes. It was a perfect day with lots of white clouds looming around 9,000 feet. So many plane rides in the past eight years, I never imagined my mother sitting next to me on any of them. Not once did I have any negative thoughts when we got on the plane or once in flight. None that I remember anyway. Even in my last moments exiting the plane, everything felt routine.

At 14,000 feet, the plane starts to stall and the green light comes on. At this time all the jumpers begin bailing. I gave my mom a hug and told her I loved her. For those doing their first tandems, this is when reality sets in, when you actually see people jumping from the plane. I was up; I waved to everyone and leaped out the door.

I jumped out facing the plane and smiled at Craig as he snapped a shot. My free fall would be just like my last, a sit fly. I went right into my sit and watched the plane fade away. As I was free falling, I watched the inlet. At this point I was getting good at sit flying. I could hold the sit for my whole skydive and even execute turns while doing so. There were some high cumulus clouds that day which I just fell right through.

Before I knew it, I was reaching my pull altitude. At 5,000 feet it was time to get to my belly. I was going to pull somewhat low so I could get to the hanger and grab the camera before Mom and Linda landed. Once 3,500 feet, I threw my pilot chute, which deployed my main canopy. The snivel process is when your parachute deploys from the bag. It takes around five seconds for your canopy to fully open. I was always taught to deploy my canopy and count to five, then look up and check its condition. Before I gave my count, I knew something was wrong. I had begun to spin violently, dropping altitude fast.

A few jumps prior, one of the packers packing my rig told me I should start thinking about replacing my lines. So the first thought was broken lines, but I did not see any. I had to act fast. My first reaction was to pull down on my rear riser that connected my harness to the canopy. By doing so, I was able to somewhat fly straight and slow the spinning. I was looking at the canopy trying to pinpoint my malfunction. I recall seeing that one of my break lines had come unstowed, which was causing me to spin.

The rule of twos applies to skydiving. You have two attempts to correct your issue and if they are not successful, you cut away and use your reserve. Still to this day I ask myself, why did this not register? I was using all my strength to pull on my rear riser, thinking to myself that maybe I would be able to hold on like that for the rest of my canopy ride and prepare for a hard landing; the amount of strength it took from me to hold my canopy steady for even just a short time made me realize that this would not be possible. I was working against nature, and losing quickly. Eventually I had no more strength and had to let go.

I went right back into a spin and by this time I realized the only option was to use my reserve. This is when I realized I had broken yet another crucial rule when skydiving, being altitude aware. I looked at my altimeter and saw I was around 800 feet. I had a decision to make – whether or not to cut away.

I had snapshots of life flickering before my eyes while spinning even faster at a terrifyingly low altitude. I am not entirely sure if I were conscious for the final seconds before hitting the ground or if I lost consciousness due to centrifugal force. Sometimes your brain erases any memory of traumatic events; either way I do not recall the final moments of my plummet to earth.

I had landed a few feet from the paved runway in the grass field just west of the main hanger. Judy, who was working in the manifest office that day, had called for Rob to drive out to the field and pick up an injured jumper. Rob Stevenson was one of the seasoned master instructors at Sebastian. Whenever a jumper lands out in the woods, or anywhere but the drop zone, the instructors have a truck to respond. Rob grabbed a radio and took Troy along with him. Troy is one of the regular jumpers who sometimes works at the Zoo Bar.

Upon arrival, they saw me lying on my left side, badly injured. Rob immediately radioed to get an air ambulance to respond; the situation was critical. "If we don't get help right away, he is going to die," was Rob's response to Manifest. He was trying to get a response from me but got only rapid gasps for air. I had blood coming from just about everywhere - my ears, nose, eyes and mouth. My right side had taken the impact. My right leg was bent at different angles with the femur bone exposed. It was difficult for Rob to communicate with me due to my full-face helmet. I had my visor up and was still breathing but with blood coming out of my airway. Rob has been in the sport of skydiving for 20 years, and has witnessed many incidents; later he told me that mine was the worst.

Rob and Troy had some medical knowledge, which may have saved my life. At some point, Troy had noticed that I stopped breathing and he could not locate a pulse. Rob knew the first thing he had to do was clear my airway. He performed a finger sweep in my mouth. He pulled my tongue back from my throat, and scooped a load of gunk and broken teeth from my mouth. He then tilted my head back to open up the airway. Rob was about to begin CPR when I suddenly coughed, spitting blood on his face. Derrick, another jumper, arrived on the scene. Derrick was a nurse; he kept me stable by holding my head in a neutral position and monitoring my breathing until EMS arrived.

My mom was still under her canopy when I hit the ground. As they made their decent over the drop zone, Dave noticed people running out to the middle of the drop zone. At first he could not tell who was injured, but quickly realized it was me. My mom was waving to her friends on the field, but they were not waving back.

My mom saw Linda standing on the field waiting for her to land. Both Linda and my mum are nurses. All the nurses have what my mom refers to as a bad nurse face. This is more of an expression when showing up to work, and something terrible has happened, usually a loss of a patient. On the final descent to the ground, my mom saw Linda with the bad nurse face and she just said "Ty." Just then, mom heard sirens and saw yellow fire trucks approaching. She knew then that it was me on the ground. Once she touched down, she struggled to get out of the harness and made her way toward me, with Linda by her side. Their legs felt like pegs from the canopy ride down from altitude, so they walked as fast as they could to me, holding hands.

Once they approached the crowd, they both noticed that I was only within a couple of feet of the paved runway. Just then they were met by one of the firefighter EMTs and he asked, "Are you sure you want to see him?" Mom replied, "Yes, absolutely." Linda said, "That's her son; she must see him!" Once my mom got by my side, she saw me lying half on my side, half on my back. I resembled a rag doll. My eyes were blood red, and blood was still flowing out of my every orifice. She crouched down by my side, held my hand, and said, "Ty, you've been hurt. You've been hurt badly. The EMTs are here, the fire department is here, you are on the ground and you are going to the hospital by helicopter." I lay there moaning like an injured animal, gasping for air. Mom stayed by my side until they loaded me on a stretcher and got me into the ambulance to keep me stable until the Helivac arrived. I had to be revived while in the ambulance. I had aspirated my broken teeth and lost my airway causing me to stop breathing once again. After reviving me, the medics did what they could to keep me stable until the chopper arrived.

My mother was then taken back to the hanger by truck. Linda's husband, Rick, was going to drive her to the Holmes Regional Medical Center, my destination. Linda stayed with me until I was airlifted out. As the medics took me out of the ambulance to load me into the chopper, I raised a hand up. Once I was in the helicopter, I lost consciousness again.

Once my mom was back in the car, she called my sister, Kelly. Kelly had been hanging out with her friend, Angie, at St. Pete Beach. They had just sat down and opened their first beers when her phone rang. She answered the phone and Mom asked to speak with Angie. She explained the situation and insisted she not let Kelly have any more to drink. Nobody knew that early on whether I would live or die. Kelly did not know much at the time, and was trying to process the little information she was given by mom. As my mom was en route to the Holmes Regional Medical center, and the Helicopter passed overhead, she began to cry.

Kelly packed up her stuff and left the beach. She would first have to drive Angie back to her house before coming to see me. She dropped Angie off and by that time got a call from my dad telling her I was alive. He also mentioned that I relayed his phone number to the ER nurse, which was a good indication that I was not suffering from any brain damage.

Once I arrived at Holmes, they had to get me stabilized. Apparently I was awake, alert and following commands, but I do not recall any of it. I gave the ER nurse my name and my dad's cell phone number. I was complaining of leg pain and right arm pain as well as jaw pain. I had lost a significant amount of blood due to femur fractures. I was given general anesthesia to undergo surgery and was pumped full of fluids that blew my face up like a balloon. I then received extensive radiological and physical examinations. Due to acute respiratory failure, I was intubated.

My initial CT scan revealed a bilateral temporal skull fracture extending into the auditory canals, which was non-operative. I had blood and cerumen coming from my ears. My right leg needed irrigation and debridement due to the compound fracture of the femur. My leg was irrigated with nine liters of saline to flush the wound. My left leg sustained a clean femur break, centered, right in half. I was wrapped in sterile dressings, 4x4s and an ace bandage from my toes to my thighs. Once my lower extremities were stabilized, I spent two days in the ICU.

Dr. Lance Grenevicki was called to give me a consult on my jaw and facial injuries. There was tenderness and a little motion in my mandible, which had been fractured, and crepitance on the condyles, which were both fractured. Seven of my teeth were broken and two fractured off the bone. The broken teeth had to be extracted. I had a large laceration under my lower lip and the bridge of my nose. I would have to undergo facial and oral surgery. The doctor explained to my father the risks of procedures involving the face along with the risks associated with anesthesia.

I was already orally intubated. Prior to my facial surgery I was turned over to the anesthesia staff where I was reintubated nasally. Multiple fragments of broken teeth were found throughout areas of my mouth and under my tongue. My right arm snapped in two places and had to be splinted. I returned to the operating room to have intramedullary rods inserted into my lower and upper right arm. I tolerated the procedure well and returned back to the ICU in stable but guarded condition.

My injuries were severe and I would not gauge the seriousness of them until days later. The surgeons told my family there was a good chance I would lose my right leg. The femur fracture was so bad that amputation could not be ruled out. There was never any question about my left leg, just the right. There was no damage at all to my spinal cord, which no one could believe. I also did not suffer any broken ribs or internal injuries. So there was no risk of paralysis—just the possibility of losing my leg, and the question of whether or not I would be able to walk again.

Immediately after the surgery, my friends started arriving to comfort my family and to see me. I was in a medically induced coma due to the extent of the injuries. Friends of mine began to show up—people I had not seen in years. My father was calling my extended family members and his close personal friends, along with some of mine. First Rob and then Jeff. Once Jeff received the news of my condition, he fled the beach and came to the hospital, lights and sirens flashing in the lifeguard truck.

The first couple of days, many people came and went. My mother and father would constantly have to give updates on my condition. Every day someone new would show up, usually an old friend from high school. The amount of support and comfort for those first few days was so helpful for my family. Every day my parents would hear how I was doing from my doctors who would say, "We have to see how he does today, and perhaps we'll consider physical therapy." Those days for my mother felt like an eternity.

Three days later on April 14, I was still in a stable but guarded condition. I was still intubated and subsequently self-extubated myself, removing the tube from my nose. I had no problems with extubation and tolerated breathing well. I remember doing this; it hurt like hell. It is all very hazy considering I was so doped up. I was kept heavily medicated and in a medically induced coma for the next two days.

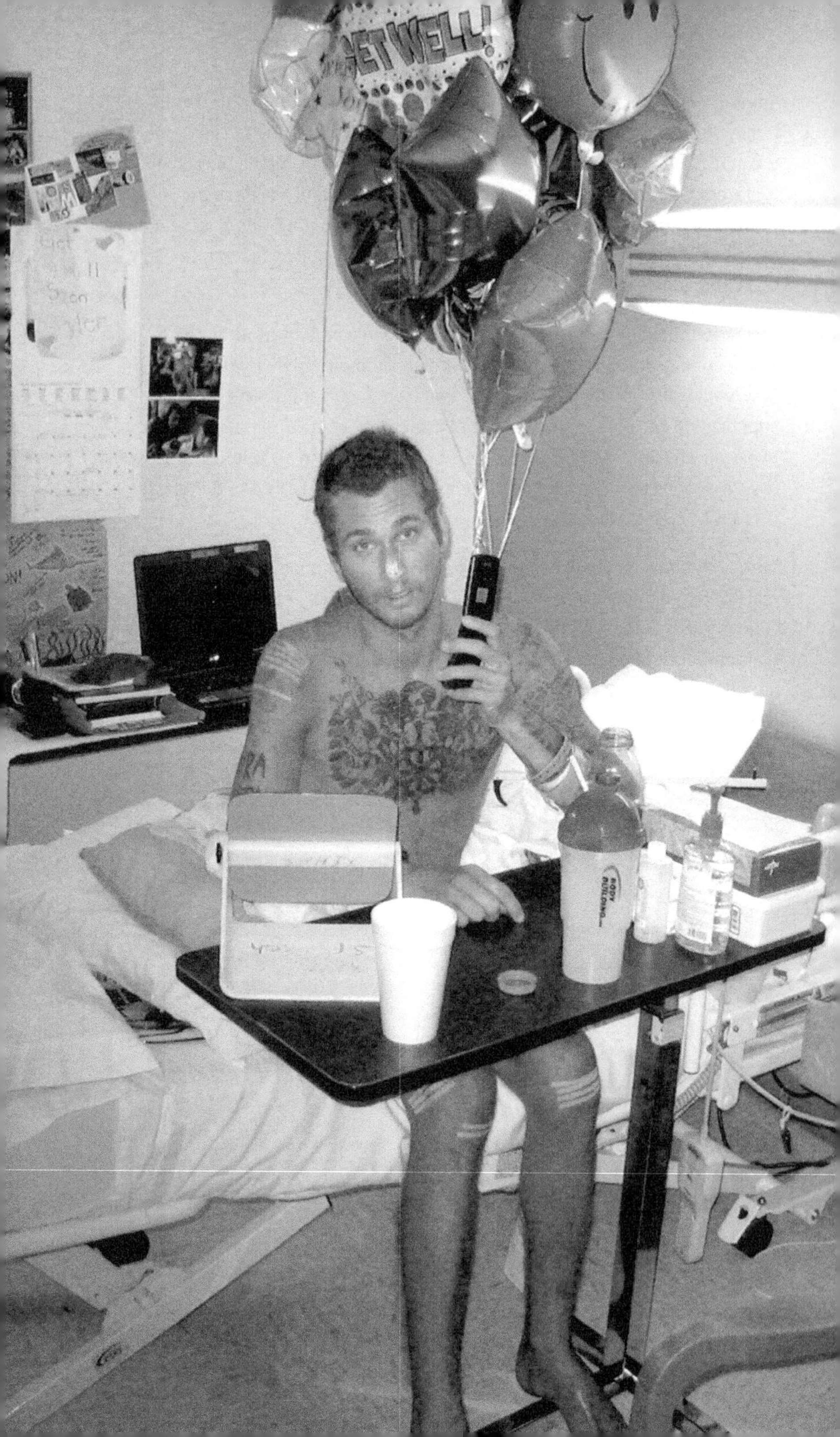
GET WELL!

CHAPTER SEVEN

JOURNAL THE PROGRESS

I was taken out of the coma on my birthday, April 16. I have some memories of that day but all are very hazy. I knew something serious had happened. Anything I said did not make any sense. I was just mumbling incoherent words. I recall seeing all my family and some of my best friends. For those first few hours I was so doped up I could not really think straight. Once the meds started to let up, I became more in touch with reality and what had actually happened. I had so many phone calls from people I had not spoken to in years, including Britney and some of my Phoenix friends. The first person I remember talking to was Kelly. I do not know what she said, or what I said, but I remember her face. I knew from that point on, my life would never be the same.

I had a large incision on my right thigh, and multiple incisions on my knees and in my pelvic region. The surgery was brand new so the incisions were stapled up. I now had permanent titanium rods in both legs. The rods were held to the bone by large screws. They were anchored in at the hip bone and the knee. I also had two rods in my right arm, lower and upper. I had multiple incisions, not just for the rods but for the guide wires they used to place the rods. My jaw had pins and screws, and what looked like a bike chain in the middle of my mandible. Even awake, I was still heavily sedated to help numb the pain.

In those first few days after my birthday, I had many visitors. It was very therapeutic for me to see friends and engage in conversation. Most visits I do not remember, but some do stick out. Garrett happened to be in town so I would see him often, along with Jeff. I vaguely recall apologizing to my mom for putting her through such a traumatic experience - not exactly how I planned her first skydive to go. I remember first seeing Lindsay. It was early on after waking up. I told her I loved her and wanted her to marry me. She thought I was just out of it, but I was dead serious. I was so in love with her and so happy to see her again. Laying there, I could not help but think of my future and how this was going to affect the rest of my life.

This was when I first met Dr. Ulises Milatano. He was young and very skilled at his trade. He walked into my room and introduced himself. "Well, Tyler, we managed to save your leg." I could just barely wiggle my fingers and toes and could not really move my legs without excruciating pain. I had been in a medically induced coma and not moving for five days, so my body was very stiff. Dr. Militano was trying to explain to me the extent of my injuries. I was incapable of getting out of bed for anything, including using the bathroom. I had a jug if I had to urinate. As far as bowel movements, I had not had one in a week. My only option was a bedpan. This was very tricky and very painful. I had to manipulate a little bedpan underneath my backside. When doing this I had to move my whole body, which was excruciating. I had little success.

That first night that I remember, I recall being woken up in the middle of the night for a blood sample. Since my right arm was broken, the nurse had to use my left to draw blood, which was completely covered in tattoos making it difficult for her to find a vein. Four attempts later she collected my blood and took my vitals. I recall waking up that first night for the nurse and thinking I was in a dream. Everything was so surreal. I could not adjust to what had happened to me.

In the early morning, I was awakened by my oral surgeon, Dr. Grenevicki. He was standing at my bedside with a strange look on his face. He is a large man with glasses, short blond hair and a face that reminded me of a high school principal. He introduced himself and asked how I was feeling. He explained my facial injuries. My mandible would heal in time, but my condyles were a concern. Considering they are not stationary bones and they work like hinges, the healing process would be a little more complex. My mouth and jaw were still both very sore. I was on a soft diet while in the hospital. I had to avoid eating anything too chewy or tough.

The first week of being at Holmes I was completely bedridden. If I did not have someone there to keep me company, I would either sleep or watch TV—there were no other options. Even holding up a book or magazine with my one good arm was painful. The first time I left my bed was on a stretcher for X-rays.

My therapist, Tyrone, was the one with the task of moving me, along with an assistant. Just transferring from bed to stretcher was very painful. Every part of my body throbbed with the sharpest, most agonizing pain. This was the first time I had moved my whole body in nearly a week.

My mother said it was even worse than my moaning on the field after I crashed. It felt like knives going into every part of my body. I was so relieved once I was loaded up on the stretcher and the pain subsided. I found a comfortable position, and was wheeled through the trauma unit wing and past nurses, doctors and other patients. We went through doors, up an elevator and down long hallways. Passing rooms I would peer in, seeing someone whom I imagined had their own life-changing experience that put them there. Once we reached the X-ray room, I had to be moved again. I could not use my right arm to brace myself or grab onto anything. I only had the control of my left arm. My X-rays were quite graphic. They displayed the large rods in both my legs and arm, as well as the multiple pins and screws in my face.

Throughout the following week, I had to endure doctor visits, give blood almost every night and wait to get transported to a new facility. I would always have someone in my room visiting, whether it was family or friends. I had stacks of get well cards, balloons, magazines and DVDs. There was such an outpouring of support from so many people. This was very important, not only to me but my family. The support helped in a way I cannot quite explain.

I went to a rehabilitation center on Thursday, April 23. I was told that since I was non-weight bearing on either leg, I would be taken to Consulate Health Care in Melbourne. I was so happy to be out of the hospital. I felt this was the first real step of progress. I spent 13 days at Holmes Regional Medical Center.

I was once again moved from my bed to a stretcher and then wheeled out of the hospital. A Coastal ambulance was waiting for me out front. The ride to the Consulate was long and bumpy. I struck up a conversation with the guy who was my EMT in the back of the wagon. He had read my story in the paper and expressed how lucky I was to be alive. I was still trying to process how lucky I really was.

I was staying in Room 400 and I had no roommates. I had a bed, TV, just about everything you would have in your bedroom, including an ensuite bathroom. I had a window with a view of a small garden and a yard. I had pictures of my sister, my dogs and my two little cousins on the window sill. My mom had hung up a giant get well card from all my friends at the Pier as well as balloons from my friends at Skydive Sebastian. I also now had my laptop and a notebook to journal in. Garrett had one of my skydive pictures blown up and I posted it on the wall along with a poster of Cory Lopez surfing Lower Trestles in San Clemente, California. These were my two motivation pieces - what I wanted to get back to. I did not totally understand how much all of these signs of gratitude, along with inspirational posters, did for me subconsciously. I would be going to sleep and dreaming of my loved ones, along with my passions in life, surfing and skydiving. Night after night, day after day, I was surrounded with positive energy while facing new challenges.

After I was all settled in, I had a visit from one of the representatives of the facility. She told me what to expect during my stay. First thing in the morning, I would be served breakfast at 7 a.m. and then go straight to physical therapy at 8. I would spend one hour in physical therapy (PT) and then be wheeled to the occupational therapy (OT) room for an hour. After OT I would go back to my room and spend 30 minutes with my speech therapist. Then I would have lunch and spend the rest of the day and night in bed. Saturdays and Sundays would be my rest days with no therapy.

The first night at the Consulate went well. I was awakened early in the morning for vitals and a blood sample, which I was used to at this point. After breakfast, I was greeted by my physical therapist, Tracy, who was about my height with short hair and glasses. My first impression was that he was very positive, friendly and comfortable around me. First thing, Tracy had to assist me from my bed to the wheelchair. We used a sliding board to do this. I would sit up, sling my legs over the side of the bed and wedge the sliding board under my butt. The other end of the board would be placed in the wheelchair. We would load from the left side of the bed so I could use my good arm. I was still in pain, but nothing like when I first moved at the hospital. Once I was in the chair, I had to have my right leg propped up. I could only bend it 60 degrees without severe pain. I had no problem keeping my left leg at 90 degrees.

Tracy proceeded to push me through the hallways, past other patients' rooms. It did not take long for me to realize that I was by far the youngest patient at the Consulate. Tracy was a young guy and I got along well with him. A lot of it was because we were close in age. Also, Tracy was an avid rock climber. He told me of some of the rocks he had scaled and how he trained at an indoor climbing gym in Melbourne. "Once you're out of here, we'll have to do some climbing." It felt good hearing him say this. It made me think, it was only a matter of time. I did not know how long, but I knew the time would come when

I would be out of there and back to my life.

We passed the lunch hall and an activities center before arriving at the therapy room. The room was very large with different machines and cots to lie on. There were lots of patients with therapists doing their own personal routines. It was all old people, and they all gave me funny looks, like who is this kid with all the tattoos.

My first task was to squeeze a big exercise ball between my knees—three sets of 10. I would do these sitting in my wheelchair. I had a hard time squeezing with my right leg, but managed to get through the 10. I felt a sharp pain in my right knee during every squeeze, so I had to find a level of pressure that suited me. From there I had to move onto a cot using my sliding board. Even with Tracy's help this was always a difficult procedure. Once on the cot, I had a bolster underneath both legs and one at a time I would lift my lower legs (from the knee down) up and hold them in the air. I would do three sets of 10 repetitions on each leg. For my first day, I did not do too much. Tracy wanted me to get a feel for everything and take the first day slowly.

The OT room was about a quarter of the size of the PT room. Tracy wheeled me in and I was met by a lovely young girl named Liz; she was going to be my occupational therapist. I spent a few minutes getting to know Liz and telling her about my accident and my injuries as she went through my file. Once acquainted, we made our way over to the main table with all the rehabilitation tools. Liz gave me a few different arm exercises and proceeded to help the other patients. I found myself gazing out the window wondering how long before I would be out in the world again, something I soon did on a regular basis.

As this was my first day, the OT was also cut short. Once back in my room, I was served lunch. Right after I began to eat I had a visitor at my door. It was my speech therapist, David. He had a list of about 15 different exercises for my jaw. They varied from puckering my lips and holding for three seconds to sticking my tongue straight out of my mouth and trying to touch my nose. I was provided a mirror to watch my progress and each exercise was to be repeated 10 times. Every time I would open my mouth as wide as I could, I would hear a loud snap. This was the hardware in my condyles moving around, which would become common. After going through all the oral movements, I was done with my first day of rehab. I ate lunch and fell asleep, exhausted.

I woke up about an hour later just in time for my first sponge bath in rehab. I still had multiple incisions all over my body, so I could not be showered. I did not have to move all that much, which was nice. I was used to being bathed this way from my two weeks at the hospital. I had never felt so clean than after those sponge baths. Not being able to clean myself made it feel like an event, or a reward... the highlight of my days.

I had a visit from my mom that night, and I told her about my day and my therapists. I knew what my routine would be from now on. It was just a matter of how long it would go on for.

The next morning was going to be just like the one before. The first thing I told Tracy when he came into the room was that I needed to use the bathroom. I knew this was not going to be easy. Once I made it into the chair with Tracy's help and the sliding board, he wheeled me to the bathroom. The toilet was about average height with handicapped bars on both sides. We wedged the board under my butt, and placed the other end on the toilet. Tracy had to lift me under my good arm and assist me in sliding over to the toilet. After around five attempts, I was finally on the toilet. Once sitting I had to get my shorts off. With all my weight on the toilet and the use of only one arm, I needed Tracy's assistance to do this. I needed a small stool to keep my right leg bent at 60 degrees. I could not let it hang at a 90 degree angle due to the pins in my knee. I had a button right next to the toilet for nurse assistance. Tracy left me in the bathroom and told me to buzz him when I was through. This was the first time I cried.

Getting back into the chair was not as difficult. I had a small incline on the board so I could literally slide down the board onto the chair, carefully. From there we traveled to the therapy room.

Tracy began telling me how he always wanted to skydive and how I should take him sometime. He was a very down to earth guy who understood my reasons for skydiving, the feeling it gave me. I really enjoyed talking to Tracy; we shared some of the same qualities. He would also speak to me in a way that not many people did. He did not question my future, and if I would be able to actually do things like rock climb and skydive. He would just casually talk to me so confidently that it gave me a feeling of hope that I would be getting my life back. I would frequently speak to him about my relationship with Lindsay and how it was affecting me. He was more than a therapist; he became a friend.

After a few days at the Consulate, I got into the swing of things. Eventually I started wearing weights on my legs, two and a quarter pound ones, while doing my leg lifts. All of my exercises were either on a bed or in my chair, considering

I was still non-weight bearing on either leg. My routine stayed the same in the beginning, considering my range of motion was extremely limited. Ankle pumps were always the first thing. These were simple; while sitting I would keep my feet flat on the floor and lift my toes to the sky. I would do three sets, which would stretch and strengthen the muscles I was not using on a daily basis. At first it seemed that all the exercises were very mundane and not that helpful. But later I learned just how important each and every one really was.

Occupational therapy was going well too. Most of my exercises were very simple. Making a fist, then a gun motion before going back to a fist. This, along with counting one finger at a time, were both little actions and exercises that strengthen the small muscles in the hand and wrist. I had to start out small, and with time work my way to more challenging maneuvers. Speech therapy was relatively simple with all the same jaw exercises repeated throughout the day. I did not have to move my body while doing speech therapy, which made it easy.

I had 52 staples in my body that were holding the incisions together where the rods, plates and screws were inserted. The day came when I had to have the staples removed. Rob happened to be visiting when a nurse came into my room and told me it was time to pull the staples out. She began with my knees. The staples in my knees came out with no difficulty. From the knees she went to my pelvic region. Under my waistline and above my leg was a tender spot and the staples were not coming out that easily. She was using a pair of medical pliers. She would tug and pull on a staple until I let out a yelp and then give me a break. I kept suggesting that maybe they were not ready to come out yet, but she insisted that they were. She took a break from the pelvic area and went to my upper arm. I had 13 staples in my upper arm that came out without much complication. The three staples on the tip of my right elbow all came out clean. Then she moved on to the large incision in my right thigh with 29 staples. This was the area on my right thigh where the bone puncture my skin. These staples were not as easy to take out, but not too painful. The fact that it was the meaty part of my leg on the outer side of the thigh made it relatively painless. After enduring 45 minutes of staple removal, she was finally done. It was then that the nurse said she had never performed staple removal—I was her first. Overall she did a good job; I was just happy that she told me this piece of information after she had finished.

I started journaling in May of 2009. I was not yet able to type notes on my laptop so I would write them in a journal left-handed. This felt somewhat therapeutic.

I noticed that my right thigh was leaking fluid shortly after my staples were removed. I had reported this to my nurse, Tracy, and my mom. The in-house doctor looked at it and said it was not a concern. They just covered the site with a sterile dressing, which would be replaced as needed. To me this was a concern and did not seem normal. I had a visit with Dr. Militano on May 8 when I would bring this to his attention.

May 5th

Today was a tough day!
P.T. went well with
2Lb weights on each leg,
Knee lifts, straight lifts
Knee presses and hip stretches
with a deflated baloon. Also
Left handed reaches.

O.T. was good too, shoulder
stretches hand exorcises and
arm flexion.

Went to the Jaw doctor today
Speech therepy stopped
today. I now wear a strap
around my Jaw, a no chew diet
and 90% of the time WEAR
THE STRAP!!!
Visitors – Mom Jonah

Barker Amanda

May 6th

Breakfast Scrambled eggs
oatmeal milk AJ Prune juice

P.T. Ankle Pumps, Knee to Foot
Lifts, straight leg lifts w/2Lbs
Left Knee hurts and shakes
when moving it. Remove weights
From left leg. Windsheild
wipers w/ legs. Knees to
Chest.

O.T. Same as yesterday!
Sat in the sun for about
an hour today.
Slept for a couple hours.
Ice on my Left Knee and brace
around my Jaw.

MOM POP Dab
Garrett Jeff

May 7th Pop, Susan, Rob, NAT
Kevin

Really nervouse about the DOC visit tomorrow. I hope its good news. If not I just need to stay Positive. Im alive with no head or back injuries. I have learned today how great my friend, are too. I am so in Love with Lindsay it drives me nuts. She is my motivation and my everything.

My Knee still hurts. Not as bad though. Sat outside today again today. I cant wait to surf and jump again.

THINK POSITIVE

STAY POSITIVE!

I noticed that my right thigh was leaking fluid shortly after my staples were removed. I had reported this to my nurse, Tracy, and my mom. The in-house doctor looked at it and said it was not a concern. They just covered the site with a sterile dressing, which would be replaced as needed. To me this was a concern and did not seem normal. I had a visit with Dr. Militano on May 8 when I would bring this to his attention.

I had a pickup scheduled at 9 a.m. from the Consulate back to Holmes to have my leg checked. My driver met me in my room and wheeled me to the exit. The vehicle I was being transported in was a big van that had a mechanical device built into the side door. My driver wheeled me onto the platform and it retracted back into the van with me on it. Once in the van, I was strapped in with multiple seat belts. On the ride over I called Lindsay to tell her about my leg and the details about my staple removal. It was so tough being away from her; she could only come to visit me once or twice a week. The times I knew she was coming to visit were always my favorite. Just seeing her face always brought a smile to mine. Her big green eyes and lovely smile would always leave me on Cloud Nine.

I did not know what to expect from this doctor's visit. I was thinking the worst case would be that they would have to amputate my leg. I arrived at the trauma center and met my mom out front. This had been my first visit to this particular office at Holmes. The room was packed with other waiting patients. Some people with crutches, some in wheelchairs like me. The wait felt like forever, but they finally called my name. I was placed in a small room to await the arrival of Dr. Militano. I felt that it was possible I may lose my leg; of course, this was an absolute worst-case scenario. Nevertheless, it made me think of living the rest of my life with only one leg and what my limitations would be. This was the longest wait of my entire life, thinking too much about the outcome.

Once Dr. Militano arrived, he checked the incision. During my initial surgery he had placed antibiotic beads in my leg to prevent infection. The fluid was not clear but not blood red. It was a concern to him that it may be an infection. He advised me that I would need surgery first thing in the morning.

Dr. Militano did not want me going back to the Consulate. He wanted me in surgery as soon as possible. I waited in the doctor's office until a room opened up; once one opened, a couple therapists helped me from my wheelchair to a stretcher. It felt like déjà vu, once again at the hospital being pushed through hallways, up elevators, through doors until I reached my room. Room 419 was just like my initial room at Holmes. I had minimal supplies with me at the hospital. No notepad to journal on, just my phone. My mom spent some time with me before going back home. I may have had a few more visitors but I do not recall.

I was awakened early the next morning for surgery. Once again I was transferred from my bed to a stretcher and brought to the pre-operating room. My mom had come back to the hospital to be there for the procedure. The pre-op room is where they ask you all the standard questions about your health. It took all of 30 minutes and then we were off to the operating theater. They wheeled me into this large room with bright lights and lots of tools. There were a total of four doctors in the room. I recognized Dr. Militano but the rest were new to me. I was introduced to all the surgeons and to my anesthesiologist. I was placed on anesthesia almost instantly and before I knew it, counting down from 10, I was asleep.

Waking up, I was in excruciating pain. I was asking a nurse for pain medication as soon as possible. My leg was absolutely throbbing, but it was there. They had to keep me in the post-operating room to monitor my vitals and overall condition before releasing me to my room. The surgery went well; I did not have an infection, they caught it just in time. Once back in my room, I was hooked up to a morphine drip. Every six minutes, I was able to press a button that would release morphine into my veins. Before I knew it, I felt great. Later, I fell asleep relatively early and slept through the whole night until my early morning vitals check.

The next few days, I sat in the hospital and waited for my next appointment with Dr. Grenevicki. I had friends and family to keep me company. The day finally came to go to my appointment. It had only taken a few days, but it felt like weeks. I would just lie in my bed and watch TV and sleep. I enjoyed having visitors to talk to instead. I was taken to Dr. Grenevicki's office by the handicapped van. Once again, my mother met me there and wheeled me in. First on the list were X-rays of my mandible and condyles. I mentioned to the doctor that my speech therapy was going well. "Speech therapy? I did not order that." Dr. Grenevicki did not state in my chart to put me on speech therapy at the Consulate, but I was anyway.

Every patient who checks in to the Consulate is scheduled for physical, occupational and speech therapy. I had severe facial trauma; thus, they thought speech therapy was necessary. It turned out that was the last thing I needed.

I had been going through a series of jaw exercises for the past two weeks. My condyles needed to heal. After viewing the X-rays, Dr. Grenevicki explained to me the results. "I am going to have to piece together your condyles with plates and screws to realign your jaw. The right condyle will be a bit more complex than the left. There is a good chance we are going to have to wire your jaw shut as well. The right side of your jaw would heal better with your mouth wired, but your left side would heal better not being wired." This was not something I expected to hear.

I also had a new garment I had to wear most of the day until my surgery. I cannot remember the exact name—we called it the jaw bra. It had small pouches inside the lining to hold ice packs and it had two Velcro straps that went over your head. It was meant to keep my jaw stable, but it also irritated me and felt uncomfortable. I would have to wear this from that moment on, all day every day until surgery. The only time it was okay to take off the jaw bra was to eat. Then after surgery, it would have to be worn all the time.

Once I was back at Holmes, I texted my friends, family and Lindsay about the results. She was going to drive up to see me before the surgery. That brought my spirits up big time. My sister told me she was driving over from Tampa to bring me one last solid meal. I had two days to eat solid, but soft food. Just one week ago, I was getting used to my rehab routine and starting to feel a little bit better. Now, I was fresh out of surgery for my leg and getting ready for another one to rebuild my jaw and potentially wire my mouth shut.

The morning before my operation, I had Lindsay with me to keep me positive. We sat and talked, about surfing, about music, about life in general. It was a lot like our first conversation a couple years prior. I never got tired of talking with her; it always felt new, even if it were the same conversation. I just liked hearing her talk. The time I would spend with her was always my favorite time. Her surfing and modeling were going great, and she was traveling more now than ever before. She was in the initial stages of a very successful career. I was so happy for her, but at the same time this meant I would see her less and less. I was sharing with her my outlook on the world we live in; it was a lot different now. I never put any thought into eating food, or going surfing. I just went ahead and proceeded with life not thinking of how lucky I was to be able to do these things. Not many people think that way, but I do now. That is the truth; before you have the simple luxuries taken away from you, you really do not appreciate them.

About a week before that, I was in the same situation, being rolled through numerous hallways passing patients in their rooms, some on their deathbeds. The journey ended in the same place, the pre-op room. We went through some of the same series of questions and then were off to the operating room. All the times I had seen Dr. Grenevicki, he was always very straight to the point. He did not sugarcoat things. This was something I liked about him. Although usually when I would see him, he would not have good news for me. This was better than him giving me false hope. Once in the operating room, they gassed me and I was out within a minute.

When I woke up, I was in a tremendous amount of pain and I could not open my mouth; it had been wired shut. I was expecting this so I was not too surprised. I immediately got a nurse's attention and mumbled to her I was in pain and to give me meds. I spent a little time in the post-op room until they were ready to take me back to my room. I was very groggy after the surgery and I looked like hell. I did not want any visitors at this point. Before I had any time to say no to any visits, Eisen showed up with some protein shakes for me. It was very gracious of him, and he made the visit quick as he knew I was not feeling too great.

I had a suction unit above my head to use when I needed it, which was often. I was missing almost all the teeth on the right side of my face, so it was the left side of my mouth that was wired. In the beginning, right after surgery, I found myself always suctioning my mouth. It was bothersome when I had to spit or if I tried to drink something and it would spill out. From this point on I would have to be on a liquid diet. I had a menu of options at the hospital to choose from. I do not recall what I had to eat while I was still at the hospital; I was too doped up.

I had spent a couple of days in the hospital before going back to rehab. May 12, Mother's Day, was my first good day in quite some time. With the assistance of Tyrone and another physical therapist, I stood on my own two feet for the first time since the accident. My dad was there but my mom had to be at work. I wished my mom would have been there to see it. My dad later relayed to my family that it was like when I was a little boy and I walked for the first time, a very special day for us both.

The next day, the therapists wanted me to move around a little bit. They helped me into a wheelchair and proceeded to wheel me outside. This had been the first time I had been outside in over a week. It was tough for me, considering I usually spent more time outdoors than indoors. It was a very hot summer day, clear skies. Perfect day for a skydive. I figured the waves were flat, at least I hoped they were. I only spent 10 or 15 minutes outside before wanting to return to my room. It was hard for me to be outdoors in this condition. Once I returned back to my room, I was greeted by one of the nurses, Melissa. She told me she had good news for me; I had not heard good news in a while. Apparently since I was able to stand and bear weight on my legs, I could be transferred over to the HealthSouth Sea Pines Rehabilitation Center. The reason I was not brought there before was that I was non-weight bearing on either leg. I had been told by some friends and nurses that Sea Pines was a great rehab center, so I was anxious to go.

I was transported over to Sea Pines via a Coastal ambulance on May 16. The first couple of days, I was still very groggy from the morphine they gave me at the hospital. Once again, I was given my own room with a TV that was on a swiveling arm to position in front of my bed. The room was a little bigger than at the Consulate. I decked it out the same as the last one with my posters and cards for motivation and inspiration. The days would be very similar to the ones at the Consulate with an early breakfast, followed by PT and OT. I would start walking soon too, I hoped.

The next day, May 18, marked my first journal entry at Sea Pines.

My first day in rehab was a good one. This was the first day I started walking. I was assisted by my physical therapist, Elba. I was wearing a therapy belt, which the physical therapists hold onto while you walk. I was using a half walker and was taking very small steps. The feeling was very strange, like having brand new legs. I would sit on the very edge of the chair, count to three and then push off with my left hand while simultaneously receiving help from my therapist. Once I was up I would take little steps, one foot in front of the other, which was more of a shuffle. Heel, toe, heel, toe, I would say aloud. My first walk was a total of 12 steps.

After my walk, I would lie on a cot and start with a warm-up exercise, ankle pumps. This was pretty self-explanatory—bend ankles to move your feet up and down, alternating feet, repeating 20 times. Next they would place what is called a bolster under my knees and I would perform short arcs for my quads. With the bolster under the knees, straighten knee and leg, hold for three seconds and repeat 20 times. Then it was onto the buttocks squeezes, at least that is what we called it. To execute this exercise, I would squeeze my buttock muscles as tightly as possible while counting out loud to three. The abduction was the next exercise. The exercise is very simple. With a pillow between the

5/18

Today I start my Journal again. Still can't bend my right leg as well as left, but I'm walking some. Tomorrow I go to see the doc for my legs. Today was a good day! good PT and OT then Lunch, Garrett and Danille came in then Nat & my mom and her friends.
Nat is gonna clip my nails and clean my ears too! Stoked!
I was hoping to see Lindsay today but I didn't. It's tough being in here due to all the time to think. Thats why reading writing, net, shows, movies & music are so great.
Just staying strong and Positive and staying focused on getting Better is so important.

legs, slide one leg out to the side, and gently bring it back to the pillow. The heel slide was the one I liked the most. This one works the range of motion of the knees. Bend knee and pull heel toward buttocks, repeat. One other one I would do occasionally was also for expanding the range of motion, mostly for my right leg. I would sit on the edge of the cot with a towel under my feet. Then slide one foot at a time underneath me as far back as I could. Finally, I would spend 15 minutes on a stationary cycling machine. Once I was through with PT, I was wheeled across the hall to OT.

Occupational therapy was not as difficult since I only had one broken arm, although I spent the same amount of time there. My therapist was Kelly. My warm ups were very basic and involved no tools. Starting with basic shrugs of the shoulders, I would then hold up my thumb with the rest of my hand in a fist, extending one finger at a time—it was a bit like counting. Then it was arms out to the side, bend elbows and touch shoulders. Arms straight out in front, turn palms up and down, repeat. Arms out to sides and cross in front like scissors. Arms out to the sides and circle forward 10 times and backward 10 ten times. Reach up to the ceiling and punch arms in front like boxing. Flip a card or a penny over with your fingers. Pick little objects out of a box and place them into another box. These exercises would get more challenging as time went on.

Once back in my room, I would slowly begin to type on my computer, mostly notes. By this time, I was better at typing with my right hand; it was also another form of therapy. If I were not journaling about my day, I would be instant messaging with Lindsay. Even though I saw her less and less, we always kept in touch. At times I would get really sad for no apparent reason. By this time, it had been over a month since my accident, so I was adjusted to reality. I would just start thinking about not surfing or not being with my girlfriend and it would bring my spirits down. When this happened, I listened to music, which would always cure my sadness. I spent a lot of time in my room, once rehab was finished for the day. Listening to music DVDs would always improve my state of mind. The Red Hot Chili Peppers Live at Slane Castle in Dublin, Ireland, was my favorite, along with some old punk rock shows from the early 80s like Social Distortion and Minor Threat. I was at my worst at this point in time. Even though I could take a few small steps, my mouth was now locked shut for the next two months. I just kept telling myself to stay focused on my legs.

I looked forward to visits from friends and family. Besides my mom, my pop would come to see me often along with my aunt Deb. Deb was always willing to help me with whatever I needed. When she heard about my accident, she was with my grandmother in Minnesota, just getting off the plane and en route to our family home. She swung right around and got on the first plane back to Florida. Since Kelly and I were kids, we would always stay at our aunt Deb's house and go swimming in her pool or fish in the nearby canal. We have always been really close with Deb. Around this time was when my dad's buddy Michael came into town to see me. Michael was a chef at the Art Institute of Tampa and is like a second father to me. I was so stoked to hear he was coming to visit. I spoke with him on the phone, and he told me he was preparing me a blended meal that I was going to love.

My friends Amber and Catherine visited me shortly after being admitted to Sea Pines. They had brought me protein shakes and a giant body pillow, because Amber knew how much I loved pillows. They also brought me a brand new pair of Sanuk shoes, just like the ones I was wearing during my skydive. Cat was the manager of a local surf shop in Indialantic and had been a friend for a few years. I met Amber through Cat a couple of years back when I first moved to Satellite beach.

Both of them were eager to help hold a benefit in my name to raise money for the medical expenses that were quickly adding up. Uncle Mike would be the coordinator of the event. Cat was going to find sponsors for the event to donate clothes to auction, along with other items. Later that day, one of the firefighters, Ryan, who I had worked with on the beach over the winter, came to visit me. He had brought me a golden elephant. This was not just any elephant – it was Sri Ganesha, the remover of obstacles. Ryan was a long time practitioner of yoga and asked me if I would like to try. I thought why not, it could only be of benefit. We spent roughly one hour doing breathing exercises and small stretches. By the end of all the exercises, I felt great. I had an overall good day with lots of visits from loved ones and now a benefit to look forward to. I was counting down the days to getting my mouth unlatched.

The first few days in Sea Pines were good ones. I liked the overall vibe much more than the one at the Consulate. Jeff and Garrett came by to visit me during my first night and they drove my truck. It had been so long since I had seen my big red Dodge. They wheeled me out the front to get a look at her. We then proceeded down a little nature trail by the road. It was not really a nature trail, just a paved pathway through a field of grass with some big trees and a few picnic tables. I wondered what I would be doing if I were not there. I had that thought quite often.

The days became very routine. I would wake up very early, around 7 a.m. I would watch old television shows I grew up on, like Saved by the Bell and Married with Children. This was my comedy fix during my liquid breakfasts. I had tried everything from blended French toast and pancakes to blended chicken and vegetables. I was given a menu and I would circle my choice of breakfast, lunch and dinner for the week, I tried everything. For the most part, I enjoyed all the food; even some of the blended desserts tasted amazing. One morning, I had liquid eggs and that was the one meal I would never eat again.

After my breakfast, I would ring for the nurse and transfer from my bed to the wheelchair. Once in my chair I would watch one of my many music DVDs to get motivated for rehab. Then, like clockwork, the physical therapy assistant would show up and wheel me to the PT room. After all my rehab was over for the day, I would lay in bed. I would usually get my sponge bath shortly after lunch. Visitors would come to see me every day, and I would either just stay in bed or have them wheel me outside. Later during my stay, I would spend the majority of my day in the wheelchair and not get into bed until early evening. While at the hospital and the Consulate, I would get bed sores on the heels of my feet and on my buttocks from being in bed for so long. Now I was trying to get into bed at bedtime and avoid sleeping all day.

During my second week, I began walking decent distances. I began with 12 steps and now I was doing small walks of 30 to 40 steps. The longer I was standing on my own two feet, the better I felt. Even in occupational therapy while working on arm exercises, I would do them standing for as long as I could. I would tire quickly standing or walking. My legs were still not used to working yet.

May 20 rolled around, my mom's birthday. Today I was getting my first shower. I had all the staples out of my neck, legs and arm. I would still need assistance from the nurse to get from my wheelchair to the shower seat. The feeling of the water splashing over my head and down my body was beyond amazing. I had not felt this in over a month. It was even better once I was done and laying in bed. I had never felt cleaner.

I had heard from a friend about a similar story to mine. A young lady who was a professional skier and base jumper for Red Bull named Karina Hollekim. She had experienced a base jumping accident, breaking her leg in 27 different places. She went through 20 surgeries and was in and out of multiple rehabs. I emailed her telling her about my accident and asked if she had any advice.

She replied:

> Hi Tyler,
>
> Sorry for not getting back to you sooner.
>
> Thank you for your mail, I just have to say wow, I´m glad you are still with us!
>
> Was your accident April 11th this year?
>
> How are you doing now, what are the doctors telling you??
>
> (I´m not sure why I ask about that because doctors have no idea...)
>
> The good thing about "us" skydivers and extreme sports athletes is that we are used to pushing limits and training hard to get there. It is amazing what the body can do if you manage to stay positive and focused and just tell it that it will be good in the end.
>
> It has taken me 3 years in hospitals and rehab centers now, with 20 surgeries, but I am walking and traveling today and will be back on skis this winter! It's been a long way, but it sure has been worth it.
>
> I think that my most important tip is to not think about all the things you cannot do right now because it will make you sad. Don't worry about the future because we don't know anything about it.
>
> Instead you have to focus on the little things in the everyday that make you happy and give you progress. It can be moving from the wheelchair to your bed all on your own, going to the bathroom on your own or spending the first night in your home bed... anything that is good!
>
> Keep your chin up, I would be happy to get some news from you to hear how you progress.
>
> Best
>
> -k-

Karina's advice was exactly what I needed to hear, and had not until then. I just kept thinking of all the things I wanted to do but could not. This would always keep me down. Once I started thinking of the little things that were good in my life, it made me feel so much better. I thought of how only weeks ago I was using a sliding board to get from my bed to the wheelchair and now I was walking. How I went from having to get sponge baths and being stuck in bed to having my first shower. All these were small accomplishments but after that email they were challenges I had overcome. I began setting very small achievable goals for myself, which would create a snowball effect for my progress in the months that followed.

Photo Credit
tropicalhainan.com

CHAPTER EIGHT

BUILDING HABITS

My stay at Sea Pines was coming to an end, and I was seeing incredible improvements day by day. Physical therapy started with me walking a couple laps around the room with the help of my walker. On my first day I took 12 little steps with the assistance of two therapists. Now, just a month later, I was walking on my own around the room. This was not at a fast pace by any means, but I was doing it, and doing it on my own. Just days before, I was given the freedom of walking in my room unsupervised. That was a huge achievement for me. This was also the first day I peed standing up. For the past two months, I had been peeing in a jug while either sitting or lying down in bed.

Lindsay came to see me one last time while I was in rehab. I was closing in on my final week. At this time I had the ability to walk semi-long distances with the assistance of my cane. The two of us walked outside to the nature trail and just sat and talked. I do not remember too much about our conversation, but I remember the day. I never told her, but she was always my primary thought while in rehabilitation. Of course, I missed surfing and skydiving, but there came a point where I knew eventually I would have them back as long as I worked hard. But with Lindsay, I did not know how long I would have her in my life. So with that thought, I wanted to get better as quickly as I could. I would think of all the things we would do together if the waves were flat and we could not surf. We could play laser tag, hang out at a bookstore, or just drive around listening to music. She was always so fun to be around; we would never get bored when we were together. She was always so outgoing and would make me smile, even at the worst of times.

Once back in my room, we just laid around on my bed watching TV. An hour or so later, I had my first visit from a few of the lifeguard captains: Iain, Troy and one of our future captains, Brad. Troy was apologetic for not coming to see me sooner. I told him I totally understood. They did not know what to expect if they saw me at the hospital. I heard this from a few different people – that they were scared of what they would see. I could understand this; when you grow up with someone surfing and being active, it can be difficult seeing them bed-ridden and sickly skinny. I did surprise them, though; they had no idea I could even stand up, let alone walk. I was extremely skinny, considering my mouth had already been wired shut for a couple of weeks. They gave me an update on how summer had been going on the beach and all the latest lifeguard drama. About an hour later, Rob and another one of my friends showed up to visit. We all hung out in my room and chatted until visiting hours were over. This was one of my best days in rehab.

My physical and occupational therapy was now focused on the challenges I would face at home. In PT, my therapist had me practice different daily routines. In the therapy room they had a car seat with a roof, basically a portion of a car. I would stand with my back to the seat, sit down, and then lift and swing my legs into the vehicle. This was relatively easy. I would mostly be getting in and out of my truck, which would be a lot easier than getting in and out of a small car. Besides the vehicle exercise, I was mostly working on relearning to walk. At first I would watch my feet with each step I took. Then eventually I would just look in the large mirror directly in front of me. There were mirrors on the walls on either side of the PT room, as well as a walking platform with safety rails on each side for assistance. I began to see the same people who were also in rehab. There was rehabilitation going on throughout the day, so everyone was on a schedule. I remember laying next to this guy who looked to be in his 40s. We were each on cots doing our exercises when we started to talk. I would always be listening to music while doing my routine, but sometimes I would not be plugged in. I told him all about my accident, then he spoke of his. He had suffered a serious motorcycle accident, leaving him with a badly broken leg, a broken wrist and a neck injury. He would always be wearing a halo and was also temporarily wheelchair-bound. I told him about my dad and how he was in a bad motorcycle accident a few years ago, not wearing a helmet. My dad was extremely lucky to be alive, and so was the guy lying next to me. I had a few other conversations with patients but mostly just focused on the task at hand, getting better. There were a few other younger people at the facility, but I was still the youngest. Sea Pines was nothing like the Consulate. It seemed that the Consulate did not have a patient a day under 60 besides me.

I found the tasks in occupational therapy more challenging, the first being the procedure for getting up if I fell and had no one around to help me back up. My therapist assisted me to the ground. Once on the floor she gave me directions for how to get back up to my feet. It was fairly easy—using objects around you, like your bed, to manipulate yourself back up. In the OT room, they had a bedroom along with a bathroom. These were simulators for practicing going about your daily activities at home. It was in the final week of my stay when I finally entered these rooms for certain drills. This was a bit like a final test before being discharged from the facility. I now had the skills of putting on socks and shoes, brushing my teeth and walking. I would do all the usual drills I had been doing since day one. But now I was doing them while standing. I was still not able to stand for the whole time but at least for a few minutes during each exercise. It was a crash course of what we learn as kids.

Next I would have to practice getting in and out of the shower. The shower at my new house doubled as a tub. I had to practice stepping over the tub and not falling and re-injuring myself. I had a couple of tools to assist me besides my cane. My cane was like a third leg or arm for me. I had a stool for the shower for me to sit on while bathing myself. I also had a handle with suction cups that suctioned right to the wall of the shower for me to grasp. Besides those tools, I had a toilet seat lift. This would fit on the toilet so I would not have to bend my knees too much. The range of motion in my right knee was still very limited; it was the worst of the two. I did well on my new exercises, not falling once.

I also worked on my kitchen skills. I would practice grabbing items out of the refrigerator, pouring a glass of milk, microwaving and washing dishes. My therapist, Megan, had me help her bake brownies, which was torture. I was not able to partake in the finished product, but I did manage to suck down some brownie mix through a straw. You really do not think too much about grabbing a cup out of the cabinet to pour yourself a drink; you just do it. All of my little accomplishments felt like tremendous victories.

It was during one of my last days when I paid a visit to a young girl, the victim of a bad car accident. She had broken legs like me. She had only been in the facility a couple of days, but was extremely depressed. I had been going on two months of rehabilitation and remembered the darkness I felt at the beginning. My therapist asked if I would pay her a visit. I made my way to the PT room.

Once at the PT room, I stood out of my chair and walked over to her. She was on one of the cots doing leg lifts. I walked over to her and introduced myself. She told me that she heard all about my story. I could tell she was really struggling. I told her about my thoughts and my state of mind on day one and how they had me walking in a matter of weeks. I did my best to cheer her up and it seemed to help a little. It is hard to explain that feeling of helplessness; nothing really helps but time and encouragement.

I was being discharged from Sea Pines on June 6, 2009. My mom showed up to help me pack my belongings. This room had been my home for the past 22 days. I had spent the majority of my days here, experiencing different feelings and seeing small improvements every day, and I was fully taken care of. Now it was time to go home and improve on my own. I began pulling the posters off my wall along with all the get well cards. I was finally leaving; this was the moment I had been anticipating for what felt like an eternity. I had an old Nike shoe box that I threw everything into. It did not take long to gather all my possessions. Once I was packed, I left my room without looking back.

I was wheeled outside Sea Pines and saw my truck at the end of the walkway. I said my goodbyes and then got into the passenger seat. Besides coastal ambulances and rehab vans, this was my first time in a vehicle since the day of my accident. It felt good being in my truck again, a feeling of progress. Once we got on A1A, my mom asked me if I wanted to go to the beach. I had the feeling that if I pulled up, I would see perfect waves peeling right in front of me and I would not be able to surf them. The reality was it was dead summer and flat, but regardless, I was not ready.

We got back to my new home. I moved into this house just a few days before I had my accident. I still had not even unpacked entirely. There were only a few obstacles throughout the house I had to look out for. I had a step at the front door, a step into the garage and multiple carpets. I had to take things slowly. If I were to fall down, I would risk re-injuring myself and possibly going back to rehab. I was told by my OT at Sea Pines, "For being the youngest person in here, you're by far the safest." I was always very cautious with how much I would push myself. Of course, I did not want to re-injure myself. On the other hand, I felt like I was getting that much closer to getting my life back.

I had only been in the new house three or four times before my accident. Our lease on the house in Satellite off Desoto was up in early April. We had to leave due to the fact that the owners wanted to move back in. It was a beautiful beachside Florida home; we really did not want to leave. A couple of friends and I moved into the new house on April 9, just two days before the jump. Now I would begin my at-home rehabilitation. I was happy to be out of Sea Pines but now did not have the constant help from nurses.

Now I would have to blend all my food myself. I used the blender to experiment. Cereal and milk blended was one of my favorites. I also blended Wendy's French fries and chili - amazing. I could only eat like this for so long though. Eventually, in the last week or so of being wired shut, I would cut up solid food into mini bite-size pieces. I had multiple metal brackets and bars lined across the teeth I had left. So once the food was all chopped up, I would use chopsticks to shovel it into the right side of my mouth, mush it around with my tongue and swallow. I hoped I would put on a few pounds this way.

During the first month of being home, I had an at-home therapist come visit me two times a week. I had the ability to move around my house at will. If I were not in bed or on the couch, I was usually in my wheelchair. While in the kitchen, I would be in the chair. When it came to going down the hall or if I had to use the bathroom, I would walk with the use of my cane. My therapist would arrive in the afternoon and stay for just an hour. I would use the spare bedroom next to mine, which Garrett used when he was home on leave from Iraq. I would do most of my exercises on the bed there, mostly the same ones I did at Sea Pines. This quickly turned into a routine.

The following day, Lindsay came to my house to see me. Everything was starting to fall into place for her. This meant she would soon begin traveling with her sponsors. I felt we were beginning to drift apart. She already lived far away and I only saw her on occasions. We seemed to be going down different paths in life. She was all I thought about at times. Growing up, almost everyone has his or her first High School sweetheart or first love—or what we think is love. Some end up marrying their first serious boyfriend or girlfriend and others move on and it just becomes a distant memory. My first love in high school was great. But she and I grew into completely different people than we were in High School, naturally. We had shared good memories, but time moves on and people change. Since that time in my life I have had three serious relationships, Lindsay being one of them. I have lived roughly a quarter of my life and had only felt this way about one girl, Lindsay.

My first week home was depressing. I was not working and not mobile, so I just sat around all day. At times, I missed being in rehab; I was once again in a new environment. I had been working since I was 15 and was not used to sitting around, doing nothing. Not having anything to do to occupy my time was leading me into a depressed state of mind. Once I was given the okay to drive, I took a trip to my old gym in Cocoa Beach to talk to my friend Crystal. Crystal managed Cocoa Beach Health & Fitness and was very willing to help me out. I wanted to work out some kind of deal for a temporary membership. Thanks to the owner, Jim, I was given a free membership indefinitely to rehabilitate.

My Uncle Mike had spoken with me during my stay at Sea Pines about having a benefit in my honor to raise money for my medical expenses. With the help of my friends, Amber and Catherine, at the Longboard House, I had sponsors that would auction off clothing and accessories. I had family and friends who also wanted to help to raise money. Mike took charge of catering the whole thing. One good family friend, Billy, was going to auction off a fishing charter. With the Cocoa Beach Pier, Brevard County Ocean Rescue and the Longboard House, I was going to have lots of help and support from the community.

The days before my benefit went by slowly. I had Lindsay at my house quite a bit, keeping me company. One week after returning home I was paid a visit by Rick Neale from *Florida Today*. He wanted to do a story about my accident. Rick asked me general questions about skydiving and what went wrong, basically a summary of the events that occurred on April 11, 2009. He took a photo of me in my wheelchair holding my bloody helmet. I also gave him a snapshot taken of me just as I was jumping from the plane. The whole visit took no more than 20 minutes. He told me the story would run in the paper before my benefit.

It was early Saturday, June 13, when my buddy Jared called me. Turned out my story made the front page of *Florida Today* and he wanted to bring me a copy. Shortly after Jared called I started getting more phone calls from friends and family who had read the paper. "Skydiver's brush with death, a whole new life for broken man" was the headline on the front page. The story ran with the picture taken of me holding my helmet. The article was a good read; I had told Rick that I experienced broken lines and that was what caused my parachute to malfunction. At this point in time that was what I believed happened, I had no clear memory of the malfunction.

June 15, 2009, was very hot; it was the dead of summer. Initially I was not feeling up to going to the event. I figured I could make an appearance and once I felt like it, dip out. My pops pulled up to my house around 11 a.m. to take me up to Lori Wilson. I was already receiving phone calls from some of my buddies who were waiting there. My mood switched and I became excited to go. I had some great friends help set up the park. My buddy, Devon, set up a couple of bouncing castles for the kids, and we had a few bands performing from South Florida. Once I arrived, I saw so many familiar faces. I was overwhelmed by the size of the crowd. Once again Rick Neale from *Florida Today* was there to get the story.

A few days before the event, Jeff ran into world champion surfer, C. J. Hobgood, at the beach in Satellite and told him my story. C. J. signed a lifeguard can, which we later auctioned off. We had tons of food donated by Sysco that was grilled up throughout the day. My uncle Mike, who coordinated the event, blended me up a seafood shake, which was surprisingly good. Having my mouth wired shut, I was limited to milkshakes and smoothies. So, for the event I had my seafood shake and some Bud Lights through a straw. Parked in my wheelchair under the pavilion, I was really enjoying myself being surrounded by such great people. I did not even once consider leaving and before I knew it, it was closing in on 5 o'clock. I had made it through the whole event: bands played, items were auctioned off a few thousand dollars were raised.

The medical bills skyrocketed. This left me hundreds of thousands of dollars in debt. In the following months, I declared bankruptcy.

After the first couple of weeks at home, I really wanted to go back to work. I missed my job so much and wanted to be back on the beach. Jeff had come up with a plan for me. He spoke with his boss and decided to have me re-write the Standard Operating Procedures for Brevard County Ocean Rescue. This would be quite a big task that would require time. Our current SOPs had been prepared by our old chief Wyatt. They were prepared for 13 operational towers, not 26. Now that the organization had been beefed up, we needed a more detailed operations manual. The plan was to take our and neighboring Ocean Rescue agencies' SOPs and develop one master. My deadline for the project was January 1, 2010.

Being at home all the time was beginning to wear me down mentally. I was constantly thinking of what I would be doing if I were healthy. I missed surfing so much. I even missed skydiving, and still wanted to get back to both as soon as I could. I craved the adrenaline rush, and had no substitute for it.

This was when I looked over Karina's email again. "Do not think about the things you cannot do because it will just make you sad, instead think of the small things every day you can do." I just had to get out of the habit of thinking of everything I could not do yet. It was driving me nuts and making me really sad at times, depression was setting in.

I remember lying in my bed with Lindsay one day shortly after returning home. I was trying to explain to her how hard it was seeing all my friends living their lives and the empty feeling it gave me. Not being able to act on impulse, taking part in what made me who I am. This was one of the worst feelings I have ever had to manage. It was also at the back of my mind that I would be losing Lindsay soon. I did not tell her this, but I felt it was going to happen.

I was so happy for her, but the reality of the situation was that she was young and her opportunities were growing and we were drifting. I knew she still loved me, but due to her traveling I would go weeks without seeing her. I had never been so sad, I was at the peak of depression. All of this was in my head, and I could not find any positives through some of these times.

When writing in my daily journal, I realized that most of what I was writing was about Lindsay and our dying relationship. This was not healthy, and I needed a change. I had a big project for work and I did not want to let Jeff down. I started writing more and more about work and my daily accomplishments. I would write about how it was easier to get out of bed than the day before – those kinds of accomplishments. Slowly I stopped writing so much about things that made me sad and focused on work and my health. My orthopedic surgeon recommended that I start swimming. Justin had recommended that I check out Gleason Park's pool, roughly five miles from my house in Satellite Beach. I had the okay to do my own form of rehabilitation from my doctors, so that is what I did. It was also during a doctor's appointment in late October when I was given the advice to try to find my physical limitations.

My life started improving drastically in November of 2009. I had ridden my bike to Gleason Park, taking back roads from my house all the way to the pool. I spoke with a cute pool lifeguard and tried to work out some kind of a deal so that I could swim there for free. She had told me she wished she could help me, but that I should speak with her boss. The bike ride to the pool took roughly 20 minutes there and 20 minutes back. Later that evening I called the pool manager and she told me I could swim for free for the rest of the year. This gave me an incentive to go to the pool as much as I could.

My regimen was very strict throughout the week. I would always go to the gym at lunch time, mainly to lift light weights and stretch. I would try to get out on the stand-up paddleboard at some point just to get in the ocean. By the end of my work day, I would get home and hop on the bicycle. I would ride my bike through the back streets of Satellite Beach. Before my accident, Lindsay and I rode a similar bike route. I switched a few streets around and now had my own route. Satellite Beach was beautiful, different from Cocoa Beach. The two towns are really similar except Satellite Beach has no tourists, no hotels and is more well kept. So riding my bike every day was not a chore, but more of a suburban adventure. My ride passed mainly through neighborhoods, one church and a school. Once I passed by the police station, I reached my destination, Gleason Park. Gleason was well groomed and peaceful. With a big fountain in the middle, joggers and bikers did laps around the lake. On the east end of the park was the lap pool. Once at the pool, I would sign in and pick a lane. I would bring my fins and pick out a kickboard. I would start out with five laps, no fins. From there, I would do two laps with the kickboard, then two laps, no fins, and finally two laps with fins. I would always mix it up a little. I looked forward to the swims. It was something I was becoming much better at. I had a day at the pool with Jeff and he gave me some tips; I was seeing small improvements and that kept me going. I would fight the sad feelings and think of happy thoughts, the things I was able to do, just like Karina said.

I was seeing Lindsay less and less at this point. I needed to do whatever I could to keep her off my mind. I spent many days in bed, alone and feeling so down. I would always find myself thinking too much. Most of my thoughts were ones that would bring me down. I had to always catch myself and try to focus on happy thoughts. Lindsay would always come to my mind and unlike before, she was no longer my motivation; now she was just turning to a distant memory and a sad one. This was a point in my life when I would have benefited from a meditation practice, although I would not know anything about it until a decade later.

December 6 was one of the first times I really felt like I overdid things. The day started just like any other, with work. My lunch break was spent at the gym. As soon as I returned to work, I walked three laps around the tower perimeter with ankle weights. After my laps, I took out the stand-up paddleboard and paddled laps from one perimeter sign on the beach to the other and back again. Once I arrived home, I rode my bike to Gleason pool and swam 18 laps. The next day I woke up with my right knee the size of a grapefruit. I had a really hard time getting out of bed. I could walk—with the assistance of my cane—but even then it was very difficult to get around, and I realized I really overworked myself. This was what I was looking for though - my physical limitations - and I reached them that day.

The next day, Lindsay came to my house unexpectedly. She had been in California for the past couple of weeks. Once I saw her, all that love came right back. I had gotten her a ring a couple weeks prior, waiting to give it to her the next time I saw her. This was not an engagement ring, just a symbol of what she meant to me at that time. We spent that evening together, watching movies and just laying together. This was always the highlight of my days, being with Lindsay.

Before I knew it, the holidays were over. January 1 brought a brand new year. At this point, Lindsay and I were still together when she was home. The problem was that she was not home that often and when she was, she did not have the time to spend with me. From the very beginning, I would always tell her, "Do what you love and follow your dreams." I would always tell her that, and I always meant it. But there comes a point when you have to let go. I wanted to be with this girl I could not have. If I would have just listened to my friends, I may have gotten out of the relationship sooner than I did.

January was the month I started to finish up my clinicals for EMT. I spoke with the EMT coordinator at BCC, and we figured out how much clinical time I had left to finish. She scheduled the rest of my hours at the fire station next to Coconuts in Cocoa Beach. I would have one year after finishing my clinicals to take my certification test to become a registered EMT for the state and the nation. My clinicals for the most part were very slow. The fire station in Cocoa Beach is one of the slowest in the county. As a student, you were not allowed to pick where you wanted to do your clinicals; it was a random decision. The only thing that mattered to me was to finish them, whether at a busy or slow station.

I had training at the end of January, and I was looking forward to it. I had finished the SOPs one week into the New Year. I was given an extension on the project from the chief, which was much needed. Now I was going to have the privilege of teaching all the rookie cadets the art of lifeguarding. I had pieced together, day by day, a solid 160-page SOP manual, which I took much pride in. In roughly four months I had finished the job I had set out to do. By this time I had cut down tremendously the amount of time I would spend in my wheelchair. My bike rides to the pool to swim were really helping me improve. I would still spend time in the chair when my leg would ache, which was often. But as long as I did not overdo things, I was capable of standing for long periods of time.

The lifeguard tryouts are the same every year. Everyone who shows up at the pool must complete a 500-meter swim in less than 10 minutes. Once the swim has been completed and the weak swimmers are weeded out, we go to the track. We conduct a two mile run that must be finished in less than 20 minutes. Once everyone is through, the times are averaged and the best times make the cut. I stood at the gates to Rockledge High School with Jeff at 6:30 in the morning, getting ready to start the day. I was so happy to be there, especially standing up and not in a wheelchair. We discussed what everyone's job was going to be, whether it was taking times or signing everyone in. By 7, we must have had 70 to 80 kids lined up. The procedure was very systematic - sign them in, throw them in the pool, take times and end at the track. From there, whoever made the cut went to the Fire Rescue Center where we conducted our SOP training.

The rookies spent three consecutive weekends in training, the same procedure I had gone through during my rookie year. We had a total of 20 in the classroom. Everyone who made the cut was a great swimmer and/or runner. Regardless, most were still in high school and not fully mature. This was going to be my first time ever teaching anything to anyone. I was still unable to work on the beach, so I was in charge of the classroom sessions. I figured the practice would be beneficial, and I would be teaching something that I loved.

The routine was simple - eight chapters that would be read and discussed aloud. While going around the room, I would jump in and interrupt periodically when I had an example or a scenario. Jeff had been teaching the rookies for years and adopted the routine from chief Wyatt. He had mentioned to me before that he was ready to hand over the reins to someone else and that someone was me, at least for the time being. The first rookie class of 20 seemed to be a good one.

February in Florida can get fairly cold; when it gets below 60, it is freezing. I am speaking as a born and raised Floridian when I say "freezing." These were the times when the beaches became desolate. We used these times to train. Traditionally, our first rookie training was in early February when the water was cold. The weather for this particular class was very cold. All the trainers had the option of wetsuits when in the water. As far as rookies go, wetsuits were allowed for all the events except the run, swim, run. This may seem cruel, but we all had to go through it our rookie year. Almost every year one or two kids drop out due to hypothermia. There is some leniency when it comes to recurrent lifeguards just re-qualifying for the following year, but not always.

First things first. Justin took all the rookies for a warm up run and swim. Justin's version of a warm up can be insanely brutal for the average human being.

He is a real beast when it comes to running and swimming, and that is why we always included him in on the tryouts. The PT started with all the rookies doing push-ups in ankle-high water until they could not no longer go on. The tryouts were meant to be grueling and challenging. We all pushed the rookies well outside of their comfort zones.

After Justin's PT, it was time for the timed two-mile run. This was the run I was going to try and re-qualify for. By this time I had been biking, swimming and running for the past three to four months. I felt very confident I would complete it. All the rookies lined up and waited for the whistle. I was lined up at the end and had my fellow captain, Iain, right by my side. Iain was our overall best lifeguard in every category, in my opinion. I respected him and admired him as he had to overcome adversity with his heart at a younger age, and came through it stronger than ever. On the whistle, we all took off. My running technique was not to run on my heels but on my toes. As I was running, I would talk to Iain and he would motivate me. Most of the rookies were ahead of me, but surprisingly I had a handful of them behind me. The fact that I was beating some of these kids really got me stoked and gave me a burst of energy. At the turn around point, my legs felt like they were on fire, but I kept running. I figured if I started walking or stopped for a moment, it would be that much harder to start up again. This was when Iain being there, and his words, kept me going and helped me finish. He kept yelling for me to keep pushing and not to give up. His words were powerful, as he wanted me back where I belonged, on those beaches with my brothers and sisters.

As we reached the home stretch, I saw Jeff with the watch, getting everyone's times. There was a small group of lifeguards waiting there to see me finish. The feeling I got from this was unexplainable. Jeff could not believe I made it in less than 20 minutes. That afternoon of February 27, 2010, I completed my two-mile run on the beach in roughly 17 minutes.

By the end of the first Sunday, the kids were all very beat up and drained. Many of them had to stay home from school on Monday to rest and recover. It is always that first Sunday that is the worst. That following Wednesday, I did my usual lunch time routine at the gym and after work my bike ride to the pool to do laps. That day Jeff decided to join me for a swim. After we both did a few warm up laps, I had Jeff time me for my 500-meter swim. I had been swimming five days a week for the past three months. This was the second time Jeff swam with me at Gleason Park and could not believe my new swimming capabilities, compared to my rookie tryout swim. For my rookie swim, my head was out of the water the whole time, absolutely no technique. Now I had taught myself the proper way to swim laps in a pool. Surfing for most of my life, and never being on a swim team, meant I had the surf technique but while swimming my head was well above the water line. Now, I had the proper technique down, and I completed my 500-meter swim in eight minutes flat, one minute faster than my rookie swim in 2007.

For the 2010 rookie class, I was given the tasks of a training officer. This was not an official position in BCOR; I was still a captain, but since I was on light duty, this was perfect for the time being. Besides going over the SOPs in class and conducting beach training on Sundays, I was also given the opportunity to help teach CPR. All of the full time guards, including myself, could tell this was going to be a good rookie class. All of the kids were eager to learn and ask questions. Throughout the whole academy, we had no problems with rookies sleeping in class or disrespecting the officers. This was going to be our second season as a full time organization, so we really wanted the best talent for seasonal tower guards.

I kept to my usual after-work routine with my biking and swimming. I would still make it to the gym whenever I had the chance. Overall, I was doing everything I could to rehabilitate myself. I was not yet back to any sports, but I was walking on my own two feet, as well as running. Lindsay was in California while I was conducting the rookie training. This was the time I needed to push myself every day and find my limitations. Simple tasks that once were very challenging became less and less difficult.

CHAPTER NINE

ENDLESS SUMMER

It was sometime in February when I ran into Donna. I had met Donna through Wyatt a couple of years back. She had always been an advocate of year-round lifeguards. During my first year of lifeguarding, I would always see her running on the beach in Satellite; she would stop and we would chat. She had made it to my benefit, but since then I had not seen her until that day at Gleason Park. She asked me if I would like to participate in her Junior Lifeguard program in the summer, and if I would be willing to speak at an event called My Legacy Showcase at the King Center for the Performing Arts. I happily accepted. My Legacy Showcase was an event that was going to be put on by special needs students of Brevard County. My part of the event would be a speaking segment called "No matter how hard you fall..." This would be my first opportunity to tell my story.

February was also the month Lindsay and I broke up. I remember the exact time she called; I was driving the lifeguard truck from the fire rescue center back to Satellite beach. It was a moment I will never forget. We had been having a rocky few months. She was traveling a lot more now and we would go weeks without seeing each other. The time I was expecting was finally there, but I did not feel ready.

In the weeks to come, everything reminded me of her. I would drive to work and pass Time Out, the bar where we first met. I would hear my phone go off getting a text message, which also reminded me of her. If it was not one thing, it was another. Being at home was the worst. My whole house reminded me of her. I rearranged the furniture, which I thought might help; it did not. I had girlfriends in the past; the relationships ended and I moved on. But with this breakup, time seemed to stand still, and time was my only cure.

I had no desire to go out and meet someone new. It was too soon and I could not show enthusiasm about meeting a new girl. Not to mention that in Cocoa Beach everyone knows everyone. Meeting someone new and compatible is not an everyday occurrence.

The emotional upset felt worse than the physical extent of my accident. I felt like my heart was pulled from my chest, I felt very alone. I do not remember ever having a feeling like that; still, to date, nothing compares. The state of mind that we are in when we go through a broken relationship can make or break our future. You must build new habits, without the company of the one you love. Those habits you may go through in a zombie-like state at the beginning, just getting by day after day. All I could do was concentrate on myself and try to get well again.

March of 2010 was the month my life really started looking up. Early March, the waves were looking fun and my buddies, Jeff and Devon, were surfing in Satellite. My doctor told me to push my physical limitations, so that was what I did. I grabbed my board and met the boys at the beach. The feeling of holding my board under my arm, walking to the shoreline, was one of the first times I was not thinking about Lindsay. I had been addicted to something healthy, and it was stripped away from me. Then to have that feeling back. I was at the beginning of the ritual as I paddled out into the Atlantic Ocean.

I never quite knew what to think or expect on that first day back, walking out into the ocean with my surfboard. I felt anxious and a bit nervous to see how it felt hopping to my feet. My first wave, I stood up with some pain in my right knee, but it was not unbearable. I rode down the line—no problem; I even managed to do a turn. I did not want to overdo it, considering it was my first time out. I could hear Jeff and Devon yelling as I caught my first wave and rode it well. This was another first time moment that gave me real hope; a hope that I could do more.

Mid-March I decided I was well enough to get back to skydiving. This was a touchy subject among my family members, not so much my friends. All my best friends, and even a few members of my family, knew it was only a matter of time before I returned to the sport. My first time back at the drop zone took place shortly after leaving rehab back in June. I had made the drive down with Lindsay to visit my friends at Sebastian. I had only seen a few of them in the hospital or at my benefit, so I wanted to show my face there and see the people who helped to save my life. As I walked up the main boardwalk, cane in one hand and Lindsay's hand in the other, the first person I saw was Jacov. It was an emotional visit. This was the first time I saw many of the jumpers who were there that day. I never had an eerie feeling or anything like that. If anything, I was overwhelmed with joy as well as curiosity as to what people witnessed, and wanted to hear as much as possible. I spoke with many jumpers and told them I would be back soon.

So there I was, 11 months later doing my refresher course to get back in the sky. Craig was my instructor; I could not have asked for a better guy. Craig was very patient and knowledgeable about the sport; we were also friends. He knew the areas I needed to focus on and areas we could just breeze over. The ground school refresher lasted roughly an hour before we were ready for the jump. The jump itself would be just like an AFF jump - a few flips, turns, some tracking and a couple practice pulls. I had made a mistake, one that almost cost me my life. I knew not to make a mistake like that ever again.

I was both nervous and excited as we loaded the plane. The ride up to altitude was not much different to any others, although I was visualizing over and over again my entire skydive. Around 10,000 feet, Craig and I verbally went over the skydive. By 13,500 feet, we prepared to exit the plane; we would be the first to jump. After spotting the drop zone beneath us, we waited for the green light to come on. Craig stood on the camera step and I kneeled down in the archway. On his count we both exited the plane. Those first seconds, that familiar adrenaline rush flooded back through me. The freefall itself felt like riding a bike—I nailed my flips, turns and did everything I needed to do. I was jumping with a bigger parachute, considering I needed softer landings and the fact that it had been so long. I also deployed at a higher altitude, 5,500 feet. My opening was clean and the freefall went just as planned. I flew my wind pattern and landed perfectly. I was now certified to jump again. Reflecting back on that jump, I feel that it was more than just another skydive; it was a great victory.

March 27 marked my first day back on the beach; I was off light duty. I took that morning to work with the Junior Lifeguards at the Hilton Oceanfront next to Lori Wilson. This was an introduction day for getting to know all the kids and instructors. Donna was there, and so was Wyatt. We did a couple demos, such as paddleboard skills, which I demonstrated. The whole event only lasted until noon. I had expected the whole day to be taken up with drills and events. Considering that we had everything packed up and finished for the day by noon, I called Jeff to see if I could lifeguard the beach for the remainder of the day. It was the first day of the season, all 26 towers open, a typical summer day in Florida.

We were fully stuffed in the north, meaning that there was one officer running each of the zones. Jeff agreed to let me ride in the Zone 3 ATV with Captain Johnny McCarthy. This was not usually how we were staffed—never two officers per ATV, not until the following summer. This was an exception considering it was the first day of the season and the beaches were extremely busy. After finishing up with the junior guards, I helped pack up and spoke with Donna about the summer and what to expect. We had planned to sit down and go over everything including my role at the event coming up at the King Center.

Johnny made it to Lori Wilson around 12:30. We did not spend much time there before heading back to Coconuts. For the most part, Coconuts was mainly crowd control. Not much lifeguarding goes on at this beach unless the conditions are very rough and we have swimmers. We had two towers at Coconuts, Tower 12 and Tower 13. Tower 13 is the farthest south and that is the tower where we were posted. We had one of our seasonal guards clear a path to the water in front of the tower. This is something that should have already been done; the path needs to be kept clear throughout the day. With the ATVs pulling up to the towers throughout the day, it is imperative to have a clear path in case there is an emergency and we need to get to the water's edge quickly.

Johnny was talking with the tower guard and I was going over the schedule when we were called by Tower 14, the farthest south tower in Cocoa Beach that Zone 3 is responsible for. "Zone 3, Tower 14—my patrol is going out for a surfer face down in the water." The way this was transmitted over the radio made it seem like a mock rescue. Mock rescues were often set up by the officers in charge to test the skills of the tower guards. But this would not typically be scheduled for the first day of the season. There was no panic in the voice of the tower guard, no emotion at all. This is how transmissions should be, but the guards are all mostly in their teens and when something traumatic happens, usually you hear sheer terror in their voices. Even Jeff got on the radio and asked if it were a mock… no response. Johnny and I did not hesitate; we hopped in the ATV, made our way to the water's edge and started heading south.

At this point, we were not absolutely sure if something was really wrong. All we could do was respond like it was a real emergency. We did not have lights and sirens on our vehicle, so all I could do was drive as fast as I could and blow my whistle to alert people we were responding to an emergency. We would have full speed on the flat sand portions of the beach with straight aways before having to slow speeds drastically with any sign of kids. We were closing in on the halfway point of reaching our tower when Jason from Tower 14 got on the radio. "Code 99! Male, mid-40s… starting CPR." Johnny began putting on his gloves and told me he would access the patient's breathing once on scene. I would be focusing on the automated external defibrillator or AED and compressions. As we closed in on the tower, Johnny took the wheel so I could glove up. We saw a patron waving us down just north of the tower at the water's edge. Our guard, Jason, had the man out of the water and had started CPR after he assessed that that the man was not breathing and had no pulse.

The man's lifeless body was still partially in the water so we all dragged him up past the high tide line. There was a small, mostly local crowd on the beach that day and a couple of local surfers helped us carry the man in.

I attached the AED pads to the man's chest while Johnny prepared the bag valve mask and the oxygen. After a rapid assessment, the AED advised that no shock was needed; we then administer CPR. I was doing compressions and Johnny was working the airway with the bag valve mask forcing oxygen into the man's lungs. My compressions were at a rate of 100 per minute and I was holding a steady and consistent pace. Those first minutes of compressions, I vividly remember the sound and feel under my palms of breaking ribs. The crowd on the beach never interfered with our pace or our efficiency.

I do not recall how much time went by before the medics arrived, along with our chief, assistant chief and police. The paramedics, in their heavy boots and uniforms, awkwardly ran through the soft sand, medical gear in tote. Once on the scene, they took over compressing the man's chest and the full duty of care. As they were loading him up to get him off the beach, he regained his radial pulse and was transferred to an Intensive Care unit at the hospital.

For the first day of the season to start like this was unheard of. The remainder of the day was quite in all zones. At the end of the shift, we had a debriefing with the two guards at Tower 14 to go over what they did right, and what they could have done differently. It was not until a few days later that we learned about the condition of the surfer.

Jimmy, 58 years old, was visiting from Orlando. He surfed much of his life, knew what he was doing, and I would say he was an average surfer. The waves were only waist high that day. He took an awkward fall head first onto a shallow sandbar, completely severing his C1 vertebra. His chances of survival were very slim, but he survived. Jimmy was hospitalized at the same hospital I was , Holmes Regional. Roughly a week after being admitted, Jimmy was taken off the machine that was breathing for him. Jimmy passed away on March 31, 2010, ultimately doing what he loved—surfing. This was a very real reminder not just for the 2010 Rookie class, but for all of us, that this could happen at any moment and any day.

My Legacy Showcase was going to be held at the King Center on April 17, the day after my birthday. I would be going on in the middle of the show. Donna was going to introduce me, I would walk onto the stage, and speak to the kids on the stage and the parents in the crowd about my accident and how it changed my life.

On the night of the event, I managed to get my family, along with a group of lifeguards, to attend. I was in my Class B attire, which we only wore for award ceremonies and special events. All the kids seemed ready to perform and I had my notes and props ready. I would have my cane, parachute rig and helmet on the stage with me. I had notes prepared at the podium if I needed them, which I did. I was wished luck by my friends and family, and then it was time to go on. Those feelings in my gut before walking out felt similar to the ones I felt during my first skydive. As I made my way to the podium, I heard the applause and saw Donna with the kids all sitting on the stage. Any nervousness I had felt was no longer there. I introduced myself and went into my story. I spoke for roughly 10 minutes before leaving the stage; the rest of the show went well.

After the event, everyone gathered in the room right outside the auditorium. I was speaking with my friends when I was approached by a woman who was in tears. She had gone through a rough time in her life when her father passed, and what I said up there really hit home for her. She hugged me and thanked me for what I had said. It truly was a great feeling that I would in later years always be in search for.

It was in April when we started the Junior Lifeguard camp. We would meet at 8 a.m. at the Cocoa Beach Pier and train until noon. All the kids were great, full of energy and really interested in lifeguarding. At times, I would be lifeguarding at the pier while they were all on the beach. I would go through all the equipment with them, showing them how it works and introducing a few of the other captains. On rainy days, I was granted permission from the pier to borrow one of their back dining rooms. I would set up a couple of Huntington Beach training videos and go through basic lifeguard fundamentals and procedures. I did my best to keep things interesting. If I could see they were getting restless, I would shake things up a bit. I played one of my skydives for them that I had filmed with a GoPro mounted on my helmet. This woke them up, but then the session turned to skydive questions rather than lifeguard questions.

The summer camp flew right by like it always does. The kids all had a blast and learned lots about lifesaving skills. It would be up to Donna whether or not we would continue the camp the following summer. I really hoped it would be continued; it was a very beneficial summer program for kids and I loved doing it. Throughout the world there are junior lifeguard programs, which early on, give kids all the information needed to understand what the job as an Ocean Lifeguard is like.

I was presented with the Lifeguard of the Year award from Brevard County Fire Rescue in May 2010. This was the first year that the Fire Rescue Center recognized a lifeguard of the year; after all, we were a full time organization since 2009. Our fire chief, Larry Collins, presented the award. Earlier in August of 2009, I was presented with a Lifeguard of the Year award from Brevard County Ocean Rescue. This has been a tradition among the lifeguards since the beginning. I felt very honored to be recognized and commended. Although the outcome would have been much different without the whole team that took part in that rescue—Johnny Danilel, Johnny McCarty, Victoria Gerace and the few 16th street beach goers that day. It was a team effort, which resulted in the most memorable lifeguarding day for me on the Central Florida coastline.

Lindsay was still always on my mind and I was constantly fighting sad feelings. I had probably 10 different musical artists I could not listen to anymore because of the memories. I knew at some point I would be able to listen to the music that reminded me of her and it would make me smile. But it was still too soon; I had to find new music and build new memories. I met different girls, but none that I really took to. I was not looking but when I stumbled across one, I would take interest and try to get to know her. Those efforts usually went up in smoke.

Hurricane season was upon us—middle of summer and very crowded beaches. This is what we train for in the off-season: days with heavy surf and the possibility of life saving rescues.

The day was July 21, and we were flying red flags due to tropical storm Bonnie. The seas were rough and there was a strong north current. Most of my day was going to be spent at Lori Wilson Park due to the large number of swimmers and beach goers. I did check my zone towers at Coconuts and 16th Street. They were good, not many swimmers – just the regulars who were mostly locals. I felt that Lori WIlson park would be the best place to spend the majority of my day. In the past, Holiday Inn was the hot spot for rip currents. This was just south of Lori Wilson. Captain Johnny McCarthy was sitting at Tower 9, the North Satellite tower, which is the busier tower at Lori. The morning was relatively slow for the most part, just a large population. Around 1 o'clock the tide was at its lowest. I was sitting by the water's edge talking with our patrol guards when I spotted a couple of girls on boogie boards close to a rip current. As I looked up to Tower 9 to alert Captain McCarthy, I realized his eyes were already locked on the two girls. Just then our Zone 2 captain, Scott, took off in his ATV to the shoreline and proceeded to enter the water as the girls were now in a rip. I went down with lights and sirens to back him up. Just as I pulled up, he had made contact with the girls. They were fine and Scott helped them to the shallows.

As I made my way back to Tower 10, I came across a mother looking for her little boy. Missing kids are very common along our north beaches. Shepard Park is our most populated beach with all the cruise liners unloading tourists there, along with anyone in the Ron Jon's area. With the crowd we had at Lori, along with the spring low tide, missing kids were inevitable. All parents react differently when it comes to losing their child. Most parents are frantic and very scared. They lose sight of their child and all they see are people and go into a panic only a parent could understand. The younger the child, the more frantic the parent. In this particular case, the boy was autistic. His name was Charley. His mom said he would not respond to his name if called. She also said he loved to swim, so chances were he was in the ocean. Once she gave me his description, I scanned the water with my binoculars. I also had the help of five other lifeguards in the area. We had no luck. Our patrol guard, Brandon, was on swim patrol looking among the swimmers. We had a strong north current so I made my way north toward Fischer Park. As we were passing the Hilton, an unguarded area of the beach, I announced on the megaphone that we had a missing autistic boy named Charley. I proceeded to give his description and just then a lady ran up to us stating she saw a young boy swimming alone about five minutes ago. We took off in the Rhino, lights and sirens going, heading north. Just 200 yards north of Fischer Park, we spotted a young solo swimmer. Right as I came to a stop, the mother jumped out of the ATV and made her way out to her boy. The tide was very low and there were lots of in-shore holes. I radioed to Scott that I was going into the water just north of Fischer Park. I grabbed a can and followed the mom out into the ocean. Once she reached her boy, she was in neck high water; naturally she grabbed Charley. There were many small and large rips that day. Charley had been swimming right next to one and once his mom reached him, they both got pulled in. Right then, I gave her the can to assist her and Charley to shallow water.

Once back on the beach, I drove Charley and his mom back to Lori Wilson. As I was filling out an incident report, we had a report of two missing 15 year olds from Lori. Almost immediately after getting a description, I was radioed by Tower 8 at Fischer Park that they were in the process of a rescue. I started to make my way to Tower 8 when the tower guard keyed in the radio and told me he was going in too. Upon arrival, I saw the patron they were swimming to. I sat on top of the ATV on the backboard watching as the guards made contact with the swimmer. I was looking for hand signals in case they needed EMS or backup. No signs were given, so I just waited for their return. As the tower guard came in through the shore break, I noticed two young boys with a couple of boogie boards fitting the description of the 15 year olds. I had him ask for the boys' names and sure enough, it was them. The current swept them 100s of yards up the beach. This is a common occurrence when we have heavy swells and bad lateral currents. At this point we had a couple of Cocoa Beach police officers out on the beach in their ATVs helping us with the missing kids. Fortunately these were the last missing kids we had for the day. Shortly after all the action, a storm rolled through, clearing the beach.

Later that day, I did a couple of interviews about the upcoming budget cuts and the ocean conditions. That evening I was on three different news channels. Fox News covered the autistic rescue; Channel 2 News covered the ocean conditions and what to expect from tropical storm Bonnie; and Channel 6 was my first interview of the day. They covered the county budget and possible cuts to ocean rescue. I figured this was good press and a great way to inform the public about what was going on in our community.

In July, I heard from some friends and fellow lifeguards that the second annual Surfers for Autism event would be held at Lori Wilson Park on Saturday, July 24. I became aware of the event just a few days before it was being held. I was scheduled to work that day in my zone, Zone 3. Our main station was at Lori Wilson so I decided to spend most of the day there.

Registration began at 7:30 a.m.; I arrived at 7. I parked and walked over to someone who looked involved. That was my first time meeting Julie. I introduce myself and offered to drive their tents and supplies down to the beach in the Ranger ATV. We would not open for the day until 10 so I had time to help. I unlocked the shed and drove the ATV to the parking lot to load the equipment. As we drove down to the beach, Julie explained her role in Surfers for Autism. She had a Learn to Swim in Five Days program for youth. She began working with Don Ryan, the president of SFA, in 2006. Once we got to the beach, most of the local community was already there setting up tents.

Derek Swor, one of our full time lifeguards in the south, had told me about the event; he pulled up right after me. Other than Derrick and me, we had one other lifeguard there to volunteer. At Lori Wilson, we have three towers and a patrol guard. That meant we would have four tower guards and at least one EMT there the whole day. We would have lots of protection on the beach as well as over 200 volunteers to push the kids into the waves. Derrick and I registered around 7:30 and got our wristbands. Shortly after the registration, Don Ryan began speaking about the day's events.

"You are all going to change lives today. The therapeutic benefit of this activity for kids on the autism spectrum and related disabilities is through the roof. This is a solid, legitimate form of therapy for the kids and for us surfers. Our beloved sport of surfing and the ocean is something very special and powerful." Don spoke about the ocean conditions due to Bonnie being south of us, giving us some heavy surf. But we did have waves and we did have blue skies! The day could not have been any more beautiful than it already was.

The Ron Jon Surf School was there to support and help out. They had brought their arsenal of surfboards and all their surf instructors. It was all about keeping a good eye on the kids and watching them throughout the day. Stay in close, do not venture too far due to the possible rip currents. Watch not only your surfer, but every little boy or girl who is in the water to make sure they come up. Then assist them back onto the board or back to the beach. Some of the kids participating in the event had not spoken a word since they were 18 months old. Some kids got dragged out kicking and screaming and were fearful. The parents requested we do it because they knew about the therapeutic benefit of the activity. Once we got them out and in the first wave, it was like a complete change from being upset and scared to being perpetually stoked.

That is when our team met Keegan. Keegan was a cute little guy with a smile ear to ear. We were introduced to Keegan and his parents and then were let loose in the ocean. Keegan had a little surfing experience so we skipped the initial coaching in the sand. Between my partner and me, we pulled Keegan out into the ocean. He had a grip on my arm as I was pulling him out to the breakers. The surf was a little overhead on the outside; the inside was just white water. We did not want to take him too far out, even though he could have handled it. As we were fighting the waves to get out to a good spot, I saw the look on Keegan's face. The look was not a look of fear, but of pure happiness and stoke. The first wave I pushed him into I rode along with him on the back of the board. He was so pumped and ready for another one. As we pulled Keegan back out, I really felt like a kid again; seeing the look on little Keegan's face was so rewarding. After a couple of waves, Keegan felt comfortable riding solo. I had to go in and guard the beaches at 10 o'clock, so I could no longer surf with the kids. For me, this was one of the most memorable days of my life. The satisfaction of working with the kids was unexplainable.

For the rest of the afternoon, I stuck around Lori Wilson to keep an eye on the 200 plus kids surfing in the water. Throughout the day, we only had two missing kids at Lori. Don broadcasted a quick description of the missing children and everyone was on the search. Both kids were found very quickly. Later in the afternoon, we had a possible heat exhaustion at Lori. Captain Scott Weintraub was already there and I responded from Coconuts. Everything was okay. We cooled the person off and gave her some water; problem solved.

By the end of the day, crowds scattered and everyone was packing up their tents and supplies, calling it a day. Lifeguards are off duty at 5 p.m. I decided to stick around and help drive equipment off the beach and into the parking lot. That whole day was so memorable for me. Later that night, I was at my house sitting on the couch watching TV and playing on my computer. Keagan's mom had sent me an email along with pictures from earlier that day.

"Hi Tyler...I have attached some photos for you of Keegan enjoying his day!! We are so thankful for everything you did for him! Just so you know, his smiles were endless and he is a very high anxiety kiddo and gets very stressed and hyper and this was the calmest we have EVER seen him!! This was truly an amazing day for our family!!! I'm not sure of the volunteer that was with you... we never got to thank her and she too was fantastic. If you see her... please tell her how grateful we are for her to be so kind with him!! You all touched our hearts in a way we can never repay!! Thank you so much for your time! Keegan keeps asking to go again! I can't wait for the next event!! If you go, let us know so we can have you help him again! He really did do great with your team!! Again, thank you for everything!! Good luck with your documentary!

P.S. The picture of you pulling Keegan with the volunteer and Keegan's back to the camera brings tears to my eyes!!!"

August was a busy month for us on the beach. We were still in the middle of hurricane season and we seemed to be getting one right after another. We were still receiving large swells from Bonnie, which took place earlier that month. I was planning on going to Daytona to participate in Surfers For Autism, but the ocean conditions were so rough I had to stay.

The day was Sunday—Sunday Fun Day as the Coconuts crowd calls it. We had our work cut out for us that day. I was leading Zone 3, and to start my day I patrolled Lori Wilson for the first couple of hours. It was the weekend and therefore we had busy beaches. People come to our beaches from all over, and unless we were being hit by a hurricane, there were beachgoers and there were swimmers. Scott was the captain of Zone 2 for the day, and he was starting his day at Shepard Park just a couple miles north. We all started getting wet and pulling people out of rips around noon. We had staffed Lori with our best guards due to the notorious rip just north of Tower 10. Everyone at Lori had gone in multiple times either for a serious rescue or an assist. As soon as Scott made his way back to Lori, I worked my way to Coconuts. I had my guards on constant patrol due to the tide change. Once I made it to Coconuts, I went on patrol with Spencer, one of our long time seasonal guys. There were not as many swimmers there as there were at Lori but still enough to keep us on edge. While patrolling with Spencer, we spotted two girls getting sucked out into the surf. I was all ready to go considering I had just left Lori and was fresh out of the water. So I grabbed my fins and bolted into the surf. The two girls were only about 20 yards out, so I made it to them in no time. They did not even consider how rough it was; they just wanted to take a quick dip and they got sucked right out. After bringing them back to the beach, I noticed Spencer had gone in for two more girls. Everyone we rescued at Coconuts that day had been drinking; alcohol and 15-foot surf definitely do not mix. This was one of our busiest days of the season. As we were going on rescues at Coconuts, Lori Wilson Park and Shepard Park were getting their fair share as well.

It was around this time that I received a notice in the mail informing me that I was going to receive a valor (lifesaving) award for the actions I took on the first day of the season. The awards were being put on by the Melbourne Regional Chamber of East Central Florida and would be held at Crowne Plaza Melbourne Oceanfront. I attended the event with Jeff and Derek from Ocean Rescue. The fire chief was there along with many other officials from the Fire Department and the Sheriff's Department. We were all given a booklet that listed everyone who was receiving an award and their individual story. Here was mine:

> In April, 2009, Lifeguard Captain Tyler Farnham suffered a horrendous skydiving accident. After several months in the hospital and painful rehabilitation, he was able to return to light duty. On his first day back on full duty, he, along with his crew, rescued a surfer who had broken his neck in the water. After pulling the surfer to safety out of the water, they did a rapid medical assessment determining that the surfer was going into cardiac arrest. He and his crew immediately began performing CPR and rendering aid until an ambulance arrived at the scene. The hospital staff later related that had Captain Farnham and his lifeguards not pulled the surfer from the water and started CPR immediately, the patient would not have survived his injuries.
>
> It was a true honor to receive this award. Everything was falling into place for me that summer. I had my life back. But I still missed Lindsay. I had not spoken with her since February, but she was still the last thing I would think of before going to sleep and the first thing I would think of after waking up. It was time to start a new chapter in my life.

NE
E
SE
S
SW
W
NW
N
20
40
60
80
100
120
140
180
200
220
240
260
280
300
320
360

CHAPTER TEN

THE VISION

"There are many of us that go through life as leaders without ever even realizing it...some good some bad. For me, I feel there were many times I could have done a much better job as a leader. As I learn more and grow, I know how to put in my best efforts to be the best leader I can be, when that time comes."

It was late June when Jeff called a mandatory officers' meeting. He had some important news for all of us, mostly concerning the nine full time captains. The Brevard County fire chief, Larry Collins, informed Jeff that he had to cut US$450,000 from the general fund budget, which is what funds all of Ocean Rescue. Having to cut that much money from the budget meant terminating every single full time lifeguard, except for the chief and assistant chief. Once Larry spoke to us about what was going on, he opened the floor for us to speak and devise a plan of attack. A couple of us paid visits to beachside hotels and businesses, alerting them of the county's plan and how that would ultimately affect them and their businesses.

We had roughly a week to do everything we possibly could to save our ocean rescue organization. Myself and Derek Swor got really involved, whether it was by sending e-mails or passing out flyers. Out of the nine full time captains, there were a select few who were truly passionate about their jobs and loved everything it stood for. Derrick was one of those elite few. He was a newer captain in the south; therefore, he would take care of alerting the community in the southern end of Brevard county.

Even though I eventually moved on from full time lifeguarding, I believe that there should be year-round coverage in this county. Maybe it is because I have lived beside the beach my whole life, but I feel that any coastal community with a high number of tourists should have trained year-round professional lifeguards. Being a citizen of this community for the better part of my life, I gained a lot of friends and knew a lot of local business owners. I spoke with those business owners and got their support.

In the meantime all we could do was keep up the good work. We only had a couple of weeks left of the season until we dropped to only manning the towers on weekends. Once school started back up, just the five year-round towers would be staffed on weekdays. Every weekend until October 31, we opened up all 26 towers. My concern was that the seasonal High School lifeguards who played on their cell phones and left trash under the towers would give citizens a reason to email the county commissioners.

This meant all the captains needed to be on point until the very end of the season. This is understandable; the citizens of this community pay for this service. When you have a lifeguard not doing their job, or doing anything frowned upon by the public, it is a concern. Throughout the year we had complaints, mainly about cell phone usage. Having teenage kids sitting in lifeguard towers all day, it was inevitable that they would play on their phones.

The better part of the summer was over and there had been only one drowning in an unguarded area. During the next couple of weeks, I made announcements on the radio about the possibility of rips with the changing of the tides and conducted more in-service training in the afternoons to keep the guards alert. All of us did our part to keep the beaches running professionally. We would also remind the seasonal guards that all the captains were evaluating each and every one of them, and that this would determine whether or not they would be coming back the following year.

The time of reckoning came quickly—July 24 at 6 p.m. I was working that day and my plan was to go straight home, change and drive to the courthouse. I had done all I could to alert the citizens and business owners that their lifeguards were in jeopardy. Now it was time to show up and support the cause. I had a 25-minute drive ahead of me. On the way, I called my dad. He had just arrived in the courthouse with my aunt and informed me that the place was absolutely packed. They said the meeting room was so full they had to stick some people in little rooms with TV monitors. A few of us went back to my house to watch the meeting live on TV.

Throughout the meeting, the commissioners would start barking at each other and disagree on just about everything. They did agree not to cut sheriffs, which won over the majority of the crowd. The topic of ocean rescue did not come up until 11:30 at night. By this time, there were many empty seats in the audience. All we could do was watch and listen. They discussed the subject of ocean rescue for only a short time until Larry Collins spoke on our behalf. It seemed as if he were "throwing us under the bus" so to speak. But the fact of the matter was that our county manager told our fire chief that needed to cut an X amount of money from the general fund budget, which came from property taxes. With our economy not doing so well and the Space Center cutting thousands of jobs, getting ready to shut down, property values were dropping. If property values were down, no one wanted to pay higher taxes, which meant cutting services such as ocean rescue. The difference in cutting lifeguards and cutting sheriffs was that cutting sheriffs only meant the loss of 15 positions. Cutting ocean rescue meant terminating the whole year-round lifeguard staff. Even after the commissioners and fire chief spoke on behalf of ocean rescue, it seemed that we still did not have a decision. The meeting went on until 3:30 in the morning covering multiple agencies in Brevard county from the sheriffs, fire fighters to parks and recreation.

Our next budget meeting would be on August 3. It would be at this meeting that the commission set the mileage; they would be deciding whether to raise, lower or keep the taxes the same. It would also be the last chance for public comments.

The day finally came and the meeting was set to start at 9 a.m. I met up with Derek, Scott and Justin for breakfast at 7. We met at a beachside café down the street from my house. Derrick informed me that he was going to speak in front of the commission. I had spoken with Jeff the night before about speaking at the meeting. He did not tell me no, just not to be a representative of Brevard County Ocean Rescue. So I decided to speak as a tax-paying citizen of the county.

We arrived at the courthouse around 8:45. This time, the conference room was not nearly as packed. It was flooded with yellow and blue shirts, though. The yellow shirts represented the firefighters who are in a union. The blue T-shirts represented the veterans. We had all of maybe 10 lifeguard shirts among the crowd. I went ahead and filled out a card to speak. This was my first county budget meeting, so I did not know the routine. I sat with Troy and Jerry preparing to be there all afternoon. Jerry was also a supporter of full time lifeguards, an ex-lifeguard himself. He had been pushing for year-round towers for many years along with Jeff, Wyatt and a few others. I left to get some coffee next door at a little breakfast place. Once I returned to my seat, maybe all but five minutes later, they announced that I was on deck to speak. This caught me off guard; I thought it would be much later. I had nothing prepared, just what I had been ranting and raving about for the past month. After a little old lady finished speaking, it was my turn.

I approached the board confidently and ready to speak. I thanked them for giving me the chance to talk. I started out by stating my name and address, and mentioned that I had been a resident of Cocoa Beach for the better part of my 27 years.

"I am one of the instructors for Legacy Junior Lifeguards at the pier. This is a six-week program where we build the character of future leaders. I work with Donna Bolinger and Wyatt Werneth, both outstanding lifeguards. I am here to speak to you today about the ocean rescue organization. When you all went ahead and made us a full time program in 2008, things went from night to day. Now we have career-minded lifeguards on the beach. We have nine full time captains and six part time lieutenants. I do not want to see that reversed. You have trained EMTs and trained lifeguards driving the Rhinos and ATVs on the beach. So now we have trained, passionate lifeguards on the beach who want to work year round. Granted, in the off season there are days when we do not have a large population on the beach, but the few who are on the beach want to feel safe. For the High School students who come out in the season to work, they are seeing the same supervisors and they get to know them and develop a work ethic. All the permanents are showing the seasonal guards the right way of doing things. Bringing this back to a seasonal program and having first responders running the show would be a step backwards; it's a scary thought having them running the zones and operating the ATVs without the appropriate training. There will be first responders driving around with basic life support equipment that is out of their scope of practice to use. I feel that it's really important to have mentors for these children to look to in this county, a county that borders the Atlantic Ocean, our backyard. It is important to have protection for the tourists on the beaches all year whether it is for two people or hundreds. It is also important to educate tourists about ocean conditions.

I feel that it is very important to keep the full time guards on the beach during the winter months."

It is not what I said that made up the mind of the commissioners; it was money, politics and what was going to get them votes, but we won the battle. Taxes were raised in Brevard County. Our jobs were saved, at least for another year. This has always been more than a job for me, it was more like a lifestyle. The beach is my office as well as my playground. Being a part of the United States Lifeguard Association and going to regional competitions—this is lifeguarding. It is camaraderie, a brotherhood with sisters; this was my job and for the time being it was my life, and I loved every minute of it.

I continued lifeguarding and making plans for when I would move on. Initially those plans were to go back to school, and work toward a bachelor's degree in leadership or possibly public speaking. Garrett would be moving to Austin to continue with school once finishing his tour of duty in Iraq and invited me to go with him. I did contemplate this, although the reality was, I could not be away from the Ocean.

In 2011, I went back to school, taking math and humanities. I was also studying for a national test that would certify me as a registered EMT in the state and the nation. In February, I took my test and passed. I also passed my two classes at the Brevard Community College, leaving me two classes short of my associate degree, which I was planning on finishing in the fall. I also began having a deep desire to travel. Over the following year, my surfing slowly improved. At one point I vowed to myself that I would become a better surfer in the years to come. The pain slowly faded as I adopted a slightly different style while riding waves. I knew that with time I would be able to venture out on surf trips again.

Lindsay pressed on with her career in the surfing industry, as well as music and modeling. She is doing absolutely amazing and will make it to the top, just like I always knew she would. I believe the paths in our life journeys are still different, but my belief in fate is still very strong. She was the girl who was with me during the most crucial time of my life. I look back on my journal entries and old letters; they make me smile. Those artists I could not listen to now bring me joy. I knew from the moment I met her that she was different than any other girl I have ever come across, and very special. I also knew that our relationship might not last forever; everyone has his or her own personal life journey, and it takes them down different roads and to different parts of the world. We all meet new people and experience new things. Growing up is all about finding yourself and discovering who you are as a person. Finding someone who you truly connect with while going through life can be difficult. When you find that person who you share a special bond with, it is hard to let them go. I believe everyone on this planet has a soulmate. Actually, finding your soulmate may never happen, although for me, I can say Lindsay filled that role during those years of my life.

My uncle, Dr. Michael Royce Lynch, was a professor in Organizational Leadership at Argosy University Graduate School. He was the one who suggested that I turn all my stories into a manuscript. Michael also wrote the epilogue to my first book, *Heart and Soul*. I could not ignore the direction my life was heading. I just needed to understand how to live my new life the best way possible while maintaining a good pace and trajectory. I gave a speech in 2011, my first official speech at Hillsborough Community College in Tampa, not realizing that storytelling would be a part of my fate in the years to follow.

There are many of us that go through life as leaders without even realizing it... some good, some bad. For me, I feel that there were many times I could have done a much better job as a leader. As I learn more and grow, I know how to put in my best efforts to be the best leader that I can be. While some of us already have the traits of a leader—persistence, goal-setting, motivation and collaboration—most of us have to learn to become great leaders.

Persistence teaches you the importance of goal-setting and motivation. When I was in the hospital, I learned about Karina Hollikim and her story. Her words about focusing on the small things really stuck with me. To then see the progress, which motivated me to stay persistent, was a true turning point in my life. That persistence when you are overcoming adversity can be used to create momentum. The outcome? When you are not faced with radical challenges, persistence becomes easier, and if used consistently can become habit forming.

One of my favorite quotes is by Thomas Edison: "Many of life's failures are men who did not realize how close they were to success when they gave up." In the years after the accident, I thought more and more about this quote. There have been many times in my life when I could have been more persistent. Working in California, or even attending school; if I had kept going through the difficult times, maybe I would still be on the West Coast. To remain persistent on the days when you are least feeling able to will reward you the most. All it can take is one good day for everything to change and for your life to head in a new direction.

Goal-setting may be the most important trait of a good leader. Having something to strive for, big or small, taches us to set long and short term goals. When you reach these goals, you are rewarded by a feeling of joy and accomplishment.

Having a set goal is crucial when leading a team, as striving to reach that goal can help to bring out your full potential. And once reached, you understand the steps which may make your next goal a little easier to reach.

I have found that having a timeline in place keeps me focused. Knowing that I have a set amount of time to reach a goal is imperative. Without a timeline, we may just be chasing goals that eventually dissolving into a mere dream.

In the hospital I was mentally setting goals, subconsciously even. Looking up at the posters on my wall, thinking of how it would feel getting back to my active lifestyle. Surfing was something I did not just want back; I needed it back for me to be me again. Having a set timeline to finish revising the SOPs for BCOR gave me a goal, and a very meaningful one that lead to personal growth.

To have those goals in place meant that I had to work through the pain and depression. Karina reaching out to me shed a bit of light in that dark tunnel, giving me a glimmer of hope. I held onto that bit of hope, which ultimately guided me out of that tunnel.

Setting realistic goals is a part of what I teach my surfing students. Our goals must align with our full potential and our capabilities. They should be challenging yet attainable. I could compare me walking again to someone learning how to surf. Staying motivated to try and try again is crucial, as there is a long progressional curve before results can be seen.

The motivation to keep going comes in different forms. When I was growing up, music on my surf videos gave me the motivation to get in the ocean, even on the days when the waves were small. I wanted nothing more than to improve, and music fed the hunger to keep me going. I used the same tactic on those rehab cots, doing small—and what seemed at the time meaningless—exercises to mend my broken body.

My family, friends, community and doctors helped me reach my goals within 11 months. Often times their doubts motivated me to prove them wrong. Doctors thought I would have limitations; I thought otherwise.

Lying in that hospital bed in April, 2009, I envisioned being on the beaches again, surfing, lifeguarding and eventually skydiving. I never let go of that vision. Even once reached, I understood that if I started focusing on an idea or a dream I would get obsessed with attaining it. These dreams and visions became bigger and bigger as time went on.

THE END

ABOUT THE AUTHOR

Tyler Farnham is a world traveler, international lifeguard and public speaker. In 2009, Tyler suffered a horrendous accident, which changed his overall perspectives as well as his life decisions. As an EMT Ocean Rescue Captain, the physical rehab meant not only walking again but getting back in shape to pass the extremely rigorous physical tests to regain his active duty status. In one year, he achieved that goal.

On the road to recovery, he revised and prepared the Standard Operating Procedures for Brevard County Ocean Rescue and went on to earn Lifeguard of the Year in 2009 and a lifesaving valor award in 2010. Tyler chronicled his journey of recovery in his first book, Reaching Cloud 9, published in 2012. As a lifeguard, he often spoke to the media about ocean conditions and water safety. In 2012 Tyler was hired as a lifeguard in Australia. He went on to serve as a lifeguard and surf coach in New Zealand. His adventure continued with surf coaching jobs in Great Britain, China and numerous locations in Indonesia.

Still learning and still growing, Tyler shares the stories of his own personal development through visualization and motivation using surfing, yoga and meditation as tools for happiness, self discipline and emotional growth.